T0354395

Order this book online at www.trafford.com
or email orders@trafford.com

Most Trafford titles are also available at major online book retailers.

Print information available on the last page.

ISBN: 978-1-4251-4355-8 (sc)
ISBN: 978-1-4251-8260-1 (hc)

Trafford rev. 08/28/2019

 www.trafford.com
North America & international
toll-free: 1 888 232 4444 (USA & Canada)
fax: 812 355 4082

M.O.S. Career Gunner
By JW Holbrook

John W. Holbrook served in the Army Air Corps from his first day of active duty on December 7, 1943, to his separation on November 7, 1945. Although this book chronicles many of the missions John flew on, it is mostly a light-hearted tale of friendship and survival in the army. These are the war stories that made it to the Holbrook dinner table and were joked about with his friends. These are the stories that have survived the years and will likely live on long after John.

John at Oshkosh Air Show in Wisconsin

To the memory of my buddies:

Lt. James S. Foster
Killed in Berlin Airlift

S/Sgt. Jessie D. Allen
Killed in action

Lt. Russell Lemon
Killed in B-25 Crash on Take-off

Robert Gregory
Deceased

To My Wife
Ethel

P PROLOGUE
Wisconsin
Survivor

I was born, one of four boys, on a farm south of Plymouth, Wisconsin, in an old farmhouse, on March 2, 1924. My earliest memory is of my mother putting me on this little potty chair that was cold to the butt, to see if I would go or not.

When I was four, I made a little boat out of wood and then went to try it out in the big steel water tank behind the barn. It was a great boat and it floated across the water, all the way to the other side. In order to reach it, I crawled up on the rim of the tank, which was very wet and slippery. I lost my grip and fell into the water. I came up for air and was able to grab the rim of the tank to pull myself over the edge. Soaking wet, I ran up to the house crying. My mother picked me up and took me into the house to change my clothes. She said, "We won't tell your Father so you don't get a spanking." My dad always got to the seat of the problem.

When I was five, my brother Don and I went to pick snow apples. We had a large tree at the end of the field. I crawled up the trunk and out onto a branch to pick up the apples. I would toss them down to Don so he could put them into the pail. As I walked out onto the tree limb, it broke, and down I went. My sweater caught on the broken branch stub behind my neck and there I hung by the neck. Although I was glad I hadn't fallen to the ground, my sweater was choking me. I couldn't unfasten it, so I put both hands to my shirt collar and pulled it away from my neck so I could breathe. Don ran calling for my dad and he quickly came running. Dad told me, "Hold your legs straight and I'll push you up so you can unhook your sweater." Soon I was free and tumbled into his arms. He gave me a hug with tears in his eyes.

In 1936 I was in the sixth grade. We were in the middle of the depression and my dad lost the farm to the bank. Our insurance company bought the mortgage from the bank and let us rent it so we didn't have to move. We were lucky. I remember that summer. In the midst of the all that was going on, we spent the summer running barefoot with just a pair of overalls and no shirt.

That following winter it was 28 to 32 degrees below zero for two weeks straight. After three major snow storms, the snow formed drifts so high they closed the roads. We had to get our milk to the cheese factory, so instead of hauling it on the trailer behind the car, like we normally did, we hauled the milk cans on a sleigh, pulled by a team of horses, through the fields. When we came to a fence, we just cut the wires and kept going. It was a long three mile trip to Zelm's Cheese Factory in Plymouth.

When I was in the ninth grade, the new Rocky Knoll Sanitarium was filling up with tuberculosis patients. The TB was traced back to the milk from local cows. We had our herd tested and found three of our cows had TB and had to be destroyed.

TB tests were also administered to humans by inserting a needle under the skin on the forearm. If the skin raised up with a dot, you could have TB. We got our TB test at school, where they lined us up, and one at a time, they stuck the needle under our skin. A couple days after I was tested, my skin was swollen and there was a red dot. It happened to me! My folks were really worried and the other students at school teased me that I was going to end up in the sanitarium. When they x-rayed my lungs they said I checked out okay. I was relieved that I didn't have TB.

In my tenth year of high school, I wanted to quit school and go into farming or something else - anything besides school! My mother, who was a school teacher, said "Oh no! You have to have an education!" So on I went searching for new ideas. In agriculture class, we learned that the three basic tools to have on a farm were a six-inch screwdriver, a pair of pliers, and an eight-inch adjustable wrench. Those and a ball of wire would fix most anything.

In my senior year, I hauled the cans of milk on a trailer behind a 1928 Chevy to the Cheese Factory. That year, I was voted president of the Future Farmers of America. I guess I was destined to be a farmer. Mr. Ardin, who taught chemistry, filled us in on the war in Europe. He said, "The way I see it, the Italians will join the Germans and they will take North Africa. Then you guys will have to push them all the way back to Berlin." His prophecy came true.

The class also made some prophecies. They said that my friend Doherty and I would go to Africa to look for a cure for the hiccups. I suppose it was because we liked to drink Miller High Life beer at the tavern in Parnell, with our friend O'Neil.

Graduation for the class of 1941 was a success. I had the record for the most times tardy and days absent. The guys in my class told me I was going to be a huge success in life because I knew how to spread the stuff that makes the grass grow green.

T HE DRAFT
   Milwaukee, Wisconsin
   1943

The summer after I graduate goes by fast. I spend most of the time on the farm with my dad and my younger brother, Don. Working on a dairy farm is a seven day a week job. The cows have to be milked first thing in the morning before starting our other chores. After milking and feeding the cows we have a hearty breakfast before heading out to the fields. We have a variety of crops to tend to, such as wheat, oats, and corn, so there is always field work to be done. We work with a team of horses to clear the fields, plant the seeds, and harvest the crops.

I always finish up my workday by milking the cows one more time. Afterwards I clean up and head into town to hang out with my buddies. So it went most of the summer and fall.

One Sunday in early December, I was sitting in the living room with my family, listening to the radio to hear if the Green Bay Packers and Don Hudson were winning. The broadcast was interrupted by President Roosevelt with the shocking news that Pearl Harbor had just been bombed.

We weren't really sure how this news would affect us right away. One of my classmates had signed up right after high school and was in the army. We were worried about him, but as the draft age was twenty, the rest of us had some time to wait and see what would happen before we decided what we would do.

Six months later they lower the draft age from twenty to eighteen years of age. In September I get my notice to report to the draft board to review my case. They rule "no deferment", for there is no need for three men on an eighty-acre farm. They give me two months to get my affairs in order. The first thing I do is to ship my six pigs to market.

My brother, Dave, who is 4F and unable to serve, has been put to work in a defense plant in Milwaukee. Ken, who is married, is a hired man on a large farm. With me going off to war, that leaves only my brother, Don, who was going to be a senior in high school, to help Dad on the farm. So Dad decides to downsize. We have a good herd of purebred cows and sell all twenty cows for $300 a piece. My Dad takes the $6000 and he buys a forty-acre farm with a nice house and hip roof barn.

With the pigs sold and Dad, Mother and Don settled on their new farm, I have done everything I need to do for my family. I have three weeks left before I have to report, so I decide to go to Milwaukee and stay with my brother, Dave.

I take a temporary job with the railroad, hand-trucking freight for twelve hours a day, to keep in shape. After work and a change of clothes I often go down to the Plankinton Arcade on Wisconsin Avenue, where the action is. I always stop by Old John before going into *The Red Room*. Old John, who is black, puts on the best shine and always tells me what is new in town.

"Freddie Fisher is playing at the *Lakota*", he might say, "and Nancy Hart is at *The Club Teras*. She comes on dancing with a tassel on each boob and can twirl them like a propeller on a B-25. She 'musta got that idea from Billy Mitchell". I step in to *The Red Room* for a couple of beers and then I'll head out to do the town.

One day I run into a recruiter from the Army Air Corps. He tells me to come out to Mitchell Field and join up instead of waiting to be drafted. I tell him I want to be a pilot and fly the new P-51 with the Rolls Royce engine. I figured that flying would be better than being a foot soldier.

The next day I take the street car out to Mitchell Field, way out into the country, at the end of the line. It isn't much of an airport, with two hangers and one office building. The recruiter is so happy to see me. I guess he isn't doing too well with enlistees. He puts me into something called a Link Trainer, which is like flying a plane simulator. I follow his instructions and he passes me with flying colors. He congratulates me and says "You'll make a great pilot! Go home and wait for my call." I don't wait long. He calls me on Friday and tells me to be ready to ship out on Sunday.

I head back to Plymouth, because I figure I should start saying goodbye to my friends. I stop by my friend Tiny Miller, who is six foot tall and weighs 225 pounds. It is early Saturday evening and he is already dressed to go into town. He invites me in to see his Mother, who is glad to see me. She tells me I am such a good boy. "You've always been such a good influence for Walter!" When we start to leave she says, "Walter, why don't you shine your shoes? Look how nice John's shine!"

We went into town and stop at the first bar with a long, red, Miller High Life sign. We shake bar dice and the loser buys the round of beer, at five cents a glass. After four or five rounds we head for Sheboygan and the dance halls.

We first hit Calumet Hall on the north side of town. We are enjoying our beers at the bar when Hazel spots me, grabs me by the arm, and says, "Let's Jitterbug; where have your been?" So I learned to Jitterbug with Hazel to the *Jersey Bounce.*

From there we went to the 99 Hall, where our friend, Jenny, is standing by the side lines. She spots us and comes running over to meet me. "You have to boogie with me", she orders. So I put in a request for the band to play *In the Mood.*

We dance a few dances and after a couple of beers, she looks at her watch, all excited, and exclaims, "I have to be in by one!" Tiny and I volunteer to take her home to 13th street, just down from Yankee Hill Tavern, a might' fine place. We drop her by her house and then stop at

Yankee Hill for a couple of beers before leaving Sheboygan. After we leave, we decide to stop at Arndt's in Plymouth for a cheeseburger before heading home for the night.

I wake up Sunday morning just in time to eat. After breakfast with my folks, I leave to go see Ethel, my Sunday girl, who lives on a large dairy farm. Her folks always get the Milwaukee Sentinel, so the first thing I do is read the funnies. Her sisters tease her that the only reason I take her out is so I can read the funnies.

Her mother serves a wonderful supper. After that we go to a movie and when it is over we head to Mike Ten's Soda Shoppe for a hot fudge sundae. I break the news to her that I have to leave for Fort Sheridan in the morning.

With tears in my eyes, I give Ethel my Christmas present. She opens it up and takes out a gold stretch bracelet with a heart on top of it. It has an inscription under the heart that says *Love Johnny*. Ethel puts her arms around me and gives me a big kiss with Mike looking on. She then opens her purse and pulls out a present for me. I open it, and here is a chain bracelet with my name on it and an inscription that says *Love Ethel*. I've been seeing Ethel for two years and I think I'm in love with her. She is the nicest girl I know. It is December 6, 1943.

We bid Mike goodnight and head to her home, for we have goodbyes to say, and I don't know when I will be back. We go into the house in the front room and sit down on the davenport. I take her in my arms and we don't know what to say, so we just hug each other and hold on tight. We kiss each other with tears running down our cheeks. A light goes on. It is time to say goodbye. So with a last kiss and hug, I'm out the front door. I get in my car, a 1933 Ford V-8 with the suicide doors, and drive down the driveway, wondering what highways and byways I will travel before I can come back home to Wisconsin.

BASIC TRAINING
Jefferson Barracks, Missouri
December 1943, January 1944

It's Monday morning, December 7, 1943, and I'm up at six o'clock. After a sad goodbye to my folks, I jump into my Ford to go to Milwaukee. I meet my brother, David, at Bush's Bar, located on the southeast side of Capital Drive. My Uncle, Eric Knoll, who is Vice President of A. J. Farnan, has made all my travel arrangements. He has left my train ticket to St. Louis with the bartender, Jack, and when I arrive he hands it to me.

The bar is lined up with night shift workers from the local factories. Now all I have to do is sell my car. I have parked it on the street so we can see it through the big window. I ask Dave's friends if any of them want to buy a 33 Ford for thirty five dollars and a ride to the train depot. Beatle takes me up on the offer, so I hand him the title. I give my brother a big hug, and Beatle and I are off to North Shore Depot, where trains run every hour, on the hour, to Chicago, where I will be processed, indoctrinated, and sworn in, before being sent on to Jefferson Barracks, Missouri, just outside of St. Louis, for basic training. There are other men also on their way to basic. I meet a fella by the name of Bob and we hit if off, so the trip goes pretty fast.

A corporal meets me at the bus stop and takes me to a barracks where I am issued my uniform fatigues and a gas mask. In a side room, it's off with the civvies and on with the uniform. I'm told to put my civvies into a bag for shipment back home. I just can't put my nicely shined-up low cuts in the bag, for I can't dance in my G.I. shoes. Heck! I can hardly walk in them. Besides, my mother would cry when she unpacked them.

They send me to the dentist and a major sits me in the dentist's chair. "Open up wide to see what we have here", he says. He starts laughing and calls to the other dentist, "Come look in this Joe's mouth!" He asks me, "How the hell did you ever get into the Air Corp?"

He starts picking around in my mouth as he jokes with his partner. "I'm an old farm boy, and the first thing we always did when we bought a horse, was to open up his mouth and look at his teeth!" I hear another big laugh as he grabs a pick and proceeds to pick out every filling from my teeth.

I have a mouth full of fillings and I spit them out. He doesn't seem overly concerned about me as he starts drilling at my teeth while his partner makes cement. In about thirty-five minutes the job is done, and he is quick to boast that it is the record for the most fillings, eighteen, in that short of time. He finally shows some concern and asks me if I am alright, but by now I can't even open my mouth!

The next day we go to the theater for indoctrination films. The first film tells us how to protect our health. The next one is about what we can do if you can't say no to having sex with someone's sister. We are provided with prophylactics— if we want them.

The last film is about the Holocaust. The film shows the gas chambers. The Jews have to open their mouth if they have a gold filling and the guard yanks them out with a pliers and throws them in a pail. After the people are gassed, they are pushed into mass graves and covered with dirt by a bulldozer. After viewing this film, we are all ready to grab a gun and go to war!

We now find out how to use our gas masks so we can save our own lives. After putting our masks on and adjusting them, they turn on the tear gas. If no one is crying we are okay. The instructor opens the door and we have to pull off our masks as we head for the fresh air, so we can find out what if feels like to be gassed.

After we finish up our indoctrination and processing paperwork, we are all herded onto a bus for the ride to Jefferson Barracks. When we arrive, I am assigned to Squad A, Flight 128, in the 27th Training Group. There are six men assigned to each little hut that has wooden sides and a canvas roof. It is the second week of December. We are singing *White Christmas*. I never knew what home sickness was, but now I do.

I head for the phone booth to call home. Mother answers, and it is so good to hear her voice. I give her my address and ask her to call Ethel for me. I ask her to give Ethel my address, too, because I don't know how to spell her last name, a good German name, or the rural route number they live on. After talking for awhile I say my goodbyes. Feeling slightly better after talking to my folks, I decide to walk to the PX to see what's going on.

In the PX, one half has what-nots, so I go into the beer part. I have a couple of beers, but they are 3.2 alcohol content and it doesn't help my morale too much, so I head back to the hut. It's quite a walk, and when I finally arrive, I find the other guys are already in the sack. The pot belly stove is going out and the soft coal doesn't last too long, so there is a chill in the air. I quickly crawl under my two G.I. blankets with my clothes still on, to help me stay warm through the night.

I wake up in the morning shivering like an old coon hound dog coming in out of the cold. I stick my head out of my warm cocoon and hear the sound of revelry rousing everyone out of the sack. Since I'm already dressed, I'm the first guy up, and manage to hit the latrine before the rush.

After chow we fall in for formation. We are greeted by Corporal Baird, who announces, "The first thing you guys will learn is how to march and how to do short order drills."

We form a platoon with the tallest soldiers in the front, ten across and four deep. After Baird feels he has gotten us trained on the basics, he decides we are ready to go out on the street. For a short guy he sounds off loud and clear as he counts cadence. Nice guy. He marches us over to the mess hall and we are put on KP for the rest of the day.

At seven in the evening, after we get off of KP, we are done for the day. I decide it's time for beer so I head to the PX. I listen to the Christmas songs in hopes they will cheer me up, but they do nothing for me. I get two bottles of beer and sit down at a table. I am really thirsty so I swig half the bottle and this does wonders to cheer me up. I look across the room and there's a sad sack sitting all alone, looking like I feel. I finish the one bottle and get up and go over by him.

"Do you mind if I sit down?" He shrugs his shoulders and I sit down. "You look like someone whose dog just got shot."

He tells me not to give him any Christmas crap because he's an atheist. "You must be Jewish," he said. "You have the suntanned skin, dark hair and long nose. I'll just call you Hyman."

I don't bother to correct him and play along. "If you say so, Abie. I think I'd better buy you another beer so that we can become buddies. After all, we are in this war together, so shall we arm together to go forth to Victory!" I tell him I like his moustache. "Your lips look you might be a trumpet player. Do women like to kiss those lips, Abie?"

"Hyman, you are shit for the birds", he says. "I think I'll have to pass on the beer while I can still walk. I bid you goodnight. See you again tomorrow!"

Late the next day Corp. Baird blows his whistle for us to fall in for close order drill so we can march to the drill field. The guys in my hut all average six feet tall, so we lead the platoon. We have trouble staying in step and it is a while before we finally get the hang of it. When we finally get going good, I take a little half step and it throws off all the men. Soon a loud and clear "halt" is called.

Baird comes up to me and yells in my face: "I don't know what I'm going to do with you, Holbrook!"

After that workout, the day is finally finished and we head for chow, and again, off to the PX for some beers. My new friend is there in the corner table again, this time with a smile on his face. He introduces himself. "I'm Kenny Foster. Glad to see you!"

"What happened, did you get promoted to PFC or something," I asked.

"No, I just wanted to show you this", he says as he pulls out his trumpet. "What would you like me to play for you?"

"I knew I was right about those trumpet lips! How about *My Little Red Wagon*?"

"A Yank knows that song? I can't believe it!" he cried.

After a couple more beers he gets in the mood and starts playing *My Little Red Wagon*. Before he finishes it, everyone in the PX is rocking. When he finishes playing he puts his arms around me and says, "Hyman, you are my buddy!"

"Abie", I say, "I'd sure like it if we can get through basic training with a song in our hearts."

One day we go on a Bivouac ten miles out in the hills and woods north of camp. This means a full pack, including a pup tent, and clothes for three days. We march along a dirt road to the campsite.

We are shown where we can pitch our one-man pup tents next to the woods. I don't like the open area, so I go deeper into the woods to pitch my tent—it reminds me of the woods back home in Wisconsin. I find a nice, big tree so that it will be warmer underneath it. I pitch my tent, dig a ditch around it and then pack the dirt around the base of the tent to keep out the draft. I pick up dead branches to camouflage my tent and rake up leaves to make a nice bedding spot. I spread my rain coat on top of the bed of leaves, and then throw down my G.I issue blankets. After chow, I crawl into my tent and settle down, snug as a bug in a rug, and go to sleep.

The chirping birds wake me up the next morning. I open the little tent flap and am greeted by rain, cold and snowflakes. How nice! Now the squirrels start to chatter and a nearby rabbit stomps his foot on the ground and hurries off. Someone is coming.

Down the path comes a G.I. dragging his field pack, taking a wide step with his legs far apart, and then taking another wide step the other way. He makes me chuckle as he makes his way past me.

I call out, "Hey, buddy, what's the matter?"

He turns around in surprise. "Where is that voice coming from?"

I crawl out from my well-hidden tent and stand up. "What seems to be your problem?"

"I got poison ivy in my privates and now I have to get to the ambulance to take me to the base hospital to be circumcised!" He looks none too happy about it.

I pick up his pack and rifle and we walk together down the trail to camp. He introduces himself as Russ Lemmon from Charleston, West Virginia. He, too, is eighteen years old, but he has had one year in ROTC. When we get to the end of the woods he tells me that this is as far as he has to go. I pat him on the back and wish him luck. He invites me to come over to see him in the hospital and I assure him I will.

Two nights later, I meet Abie at the PX for beer. I tell him about my bivouac in the woods and about meeting my new buddy, Lemmon. I am planning to go over to the hospital to see him and I ask Abie if he wants to go along and meet him. As he has nothing better to do, he agrees to go with me. We drink up and head over to the hospital to find out what sack he is in.

This nice nurse says she'll show us where he is at. With a big smile, she tells us that Russ is such a honey. She wakes him up to tell him he has

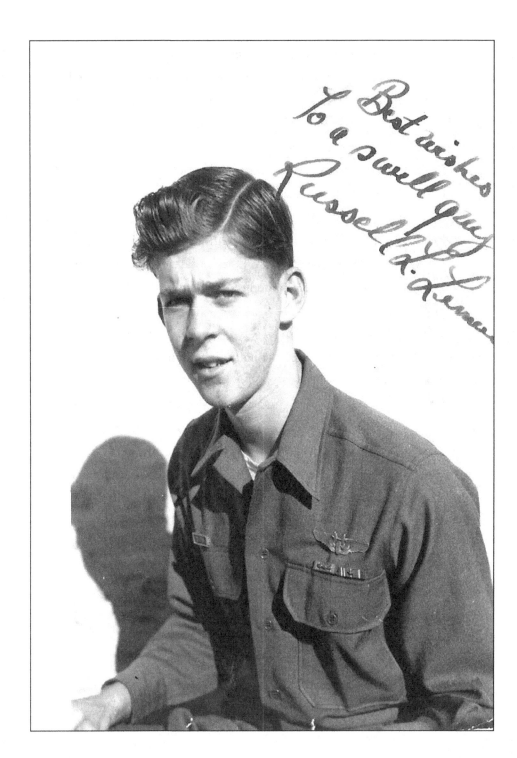

company, and as she leans over, her breast falls onto his arm. "You just wait," he tells the nurse. "I'll take care of you when I get these stitches taken out."

Lemmon is glad to see us. I introduce my buddy as James "Abie" Foster and myself as John "Hyman" Holbrook. "We're two good Jewish boys here to cheer you up," we told him. Abie has his horn with him, so I asked Lemmon what he wants to hear.

Abie tells us, "Don't ask me to play any Christmas songs because I'm an Atheist."

"Well, I'm a Fatalist," Lemmon countered. "When your number's up, that's it, you're gone. And if you have a soul, that goes with you."

"Hey Abie," I cried. "Let's get some water and baptize him so he will unite with us." I grabbed some water. "First we need a name. I know, let's call him Sol Lemmonstein." So we baptize him. "I, Father Hyman, proclaim that Abie, Sol, and I will stick together throughout this tour of duty in Uncle Sam's army." The deal is sealed!

It's January 2, 1944. We are moved to Tent City, or as it is called there, Pneumonia Gulch. I guess that is so we get used to living in a tent with flaps and tie downs. We now have a new leader, Corporal Collier, a pro golfer. He is supposed to teach us short order drills and how to march in the parade that goes past the reviewing stand to impress the brass.

He marches us out into the woods to a nice open spot where we sit around in a circle. He picks up a tree branch that looks like a golf club and shows us how he won honors in a tournament. I like this guy. We march back to camp in time for chow. In the afternoon we pack our gear to get ready for a twenty-four mile hike we will be taking tomorrow on a little old country road north of the camp.

The next morning we are greeted by a cold, drizzly rain with snow flakes mixed in. After breakfast, Collier has us assemble single file with ten men on one side of the road and ten men on the other side, but about ten feet back, so we are staggered as we march out of camp. Every hour we stop and rest for ten minutes. "Smoke 'em if you got 'em!"

After a long and tiring day of marching we arrive back at the camp. At about 1300 hours we are lined up at the mess tent for dinner. We listen to each other moan and groan about our sore feet, tired legs, and what not. We fall in for chow and the lieutenant stands on the hard stand and says smartly, "If you want to march back to the base, I'll give you a pass to go into town."

No one else seems too interested in this proposition, but I am never one to pass up a chance to go dancing. I take him up on the offered pass and I end up walking back to town by myself.

A few days later, we are informed that basic training is over. After we have packed our gear, we are brought to the train station, where we file onto the troop train. We all assume we are headed to wherever Cadets go for pilot training. We are unaware of the surprise waiting for us in Las Vegas.

Tail gunner ready for action

GUNNERY SCHOOL
Las Vegas, Nevada
February and March 1944

In Las Vegas we are met at the train station by an officer who lines us up. He immediately breaks the news to us. "You guys thought you were going to be pilots, but you're not. You guys are going to be gunners, and every one of you are here for six weeks of gunnery school. When your training is complete you will each be promoted to PFC and get a fifteen day delayed en route so that you can go home before going overseas."

I was not happy about this piece of news, and neither was anyone else. It seems they have enough pilots but they are short on gunners because they keep getting shot down, and they need a fresh supply to take their place. We protest, but in Uncle Sam's Army, it does no good. Like it or not, we are about to become gunners.

The first thing they do is put us in a preflight simulator to see how well we can physically handle higher altitudes. Once we are in the decompression chamber they start to change the oxygen level to simulate different altitudes. Once we get up to nine or ten thousand feet we are suppose to put our oxygen masks on so we don't pass out. About this time my front tooth starts to hurt, so they bring us "back down". They immediately send me to the dentist.

After an x-ray of my mouth, they determine there is an air pocket under my front tooth that is causing swelling up on the nerve. The dentist comes in and pronounces, "We need to pull your front tooth."

I have a pronouncement of my own. "Oh no you don't!"

They call in the captain in charge and he tells me that they need me up and flying. Period. "Pull the tooth," he says, leaving no room for argument.

Because I now have a hole where my front tooth used to be, I can't talk without a lisp. The men in my barracks tell me I talk like a queer. For a week the men jeer at me and every time they see me they say "Hey, Holbrook—talk to me!" I am relieved when my mouth is finally healed enough so they can cement in a new front tooth.

Before we can shoot our 50 caliber machine guns we have to learn how to quickly take them apart and put them back together. After doing this four or five times they figure we are ready to shoot at a target.

They put us, four at a time, into the back of a pick-up. The first step in teaching us how to be gunners is to teach us how to shoot at a moving target, so we shoot at clay pigeons as the truck drives around the track. The trick, they tell us, is to shoot behind the target because the bullets will move with us. We use a shot gun with a camera attached to it. The camera records our hits and misses as we shoot at the clay pigeons. We all take turns shooting the gun as the truck drives around the course. Foster and Lemmon have never shot a gun before and they have a hard time getting used to the gun's recoil. By the time we are done, their arms are pretty sore!

The next phase is actually going up in the B-17s. We use colored bullets and we are each assigned a different color so that they can tell who is hitting the target. I have red bullets. Again there is a camera that records how we do. We fly up and rendezvous with another B-17 that is pulling a tow target, which is like a cloth banner. We take turns shooting at the tow target and the colored bullets make it easy to identify who is hitting and who is missing the target. I managed to put in four or five hits.

Every day we learn a little more and every day we work hard. But we also play hard. We like to head into downtown Vegas, but as we only make $21 a month, most of the guys are often short of cash. Before I left home I had sold my pigs, my car, and earned some extra money at the rail yard, so I started my military career with $400. The money is in twenty dollar bills, which I have stashed all over the place. I always carry at least one spare twenty in my hat.

When the guys have spare cash we get a group together, but when cash is tight, I grab one of my twenties and head into Vegas alone. I catch the bus from base at 0400 hours for the 20 minute trip into town. The mission is usually to go to the *Lost Frontier* Casino and get lost. I'll cash in a twenty and get some nickels, dimes and quarters to feed to the slot machines and some chips to play Blackjack and Poker. Then I make the rounds. I am usually fairly lucky at Black Jack, and if I sit to the right of the poker dealer I do okay at poker. Overall I manage to have fun and still hang onto my $400. The last bus heads back to the base at 0100 and I always make sure I am on it. I need to hit the sack and relax on Sunday, so I can start all over on Monday.

Our last day of school is April 8, 1944, and we are told to meet in the post theater. First Lieutenant McCann gives us the good news. "You have all graduated from gunnery school and are now officially promoted to

Private First Class. Here are your stripes. Get them sewn on.! Congratulations. You men are the first class to graduate as M.O.S. 611 Carrier Gunners."

Now for the bad news. Your 15 day delayed en route has been canceled. You have tonight to pack your gear. Tomorrow morning after breakfast the train will be back at the station and you will depart at 0800 hours for Lincoln, Nebraska. There you will be assigned to a crew for training on a B-17 bomber. Any questions?"

We all sit there in silence. It is so quiet you could hear a pin drop. As we look at one another we realize we got the shaft (again) and we can feel it up to our stomachs. It's bad enough we didn't get to be pilots, now our promised leaves have been canceled and we will not be able to go home and see our families before being sent overseas. A loud voice sounds off, "All together men!" With loud voices we cry out, "Some shit!" I think they can hear us in downtown Vegas. I turn to my two buddies and we exchange a look. This is not good.

"Abie, Sol, we must go find our little boy, Bob." Bob is the fella I met on the bus to basic training. When I first introduced him to Abie and Sol, they immediately had christened him Brother Bob. He is a ball turret gunner, but he won't be shipping out with us tomorrow. We find Bob sitting on his sack and his face is way down to the floor. He must have heard the news.

"Robert. Good news! We are going to take you into Vegas for a T-bone steak dinner, your choice of drinks, and money to play the slot machines. It will be a night out. This will be our way of saying goodbye to Vegas like a bad dream!" I wasn't worried about the money, as my brother, David, had sent me some from Milwaukee. I left to pick up our four passes from J.D. Adams, who has a friend in the orderly room.

We grab the six o'clock bus for Vegas. A little old lady gives Bob

the fourth degree as we ride into town. "Such a nice little boy! Why did
you run away from home and join the army?" Of course we three good
Jewish boys never let him forget this.

We do some bar hopping and try to mingle with the girls wearing
the fancy fur coats, but they don't seem to like us much. We wind up at the
Lost Frontier for the steak dinner we promised Bob. We top off our full
stomachs with a few beers. After an hour or two, I can tell that the guys
can't hold their beer like the guys back in Wisconsin, so I herd them to the
bus and back to camp.

About midnight we find our barracks and go in singing, "Mares eat
oats and little lambs eat ivy." Now before we can hit the sack we must
repeat the Gunner's vow. "All together men!"

I wish to be a pilot and you along with me.
But if we were all pilots, we would the Air Force be.
It takes guts to be a gunner, to sit out on the tail
When the Messerschmitts are coming and the slugs begin to wail.
The pilot's just a chauffeur. It's his job to fly the plane.
But it's we who do the fighting, though we may not get the fame.
If we all must be gunners, let us make this bet.
We'll be the best damn gunners who have left Las Vegas yet!

We loudly clap our hands and cheer as a loud voice yells, "You guys
are nuts! You're going to be the first to get shot down!"

So we sing to him *Goodnight Sweetheart,* and tuck him in before we
crawl into our own sacks.

CREW ASSIGNMENTS
Lincoln, Nebraska
April 1944

We take the train from Las Vegas to Lincoln. At the depot in Lincoln, we are met by a sergeant and a lieutenant. We fall into formation and march to the barracks. The lieutenant gets up on the steps and gives us the standard welcome.

"When your name is called, the sergeant will take your orders and then you can go into the barracks. He will also give you a courtesy card! On the back are the rules that you are to follow at this camp. Read them! If you break one of these rules, you will face disciplinary action. Have a good night!"

The bugle sounds at 0600 hours. We fall out and head for the mess hall. We sleep with our clothes on so that we will be first in line. The cook looks surprised. "How the hell did you PFC's get in line so fast? We just opened up. You three look like trouble to me!"

Being a good boy I simply said, "Have a nice day. Don't burn yourself!"

The food looks good and we chow down because we are hungry. As we are eating, we try to figure out how we are going to get the same shipping orders so we won't get split up. We have heard that the screw-ups get shipped out first and then everyone else gets shipped out in alphabetical order.

We pull out our courtesy cards with all the rules on them. The first one says that the PX is off limits to enlisted men from 0900 to 1600 hours. We formulate a plan of action.

We decide that we need to get everyone's attention, so we first mess with our clothing. We put on our Officer-of-the-Day caps, fatigue shirts with PFC strips on them, and then our dress pants. At 0900 hours, we walk into the PX and sit down at the table by the window so those who walk past us will get a big laugh. We order BLTs and are enjoying them when a lieutenant walks by. He can't believe his eyes! He marches straight towards us and demands that we show him our courtesy cards.

"You had better eat up, because if you are not out of here in ten minutes I am calling the MPs!" I didn't know that lieutenants could get so red in the face! We quickly finish up our breakfast and leave.

Back at the barracks, we check out the bulletin board so we can see what's going on. We see there is a big formation at 0800 hours tomorrow morning. We decide it would be a good day to sleep in so we will get another mark on our courtesy cards.

The next morning at 0900 hours we are awakened by an angry captain barking at us to get dressed. "Put on your dress shirt with your PFC stripes." He waits until we are ready. "Follow me," he barks again.

We crawl up onto the viewing stand in front of the formation. The captain shouts out, "These three were asleep in their bunks instead of in formation. I'm going to see that these men are reduced to privates," and with that, he yanks the stripes off our shirts. "Be out in front of your barracks tomorrow at 0900 hours for your punishment. And let this be a lesson to you new men!"

Our boys in the ranks raise a cheer, "All together men. Chicken shit! Chicken shit! Chicken Shit!" All the men are laughing as the captain walks off the stage.

The next morning, we are standing in the rain as we wait for the MPs to arrive, each of us wearing a heavy seat pack and our backpacks. The rain is coming down hard and is making big puddles in the worn street. The MPs arrive and take us down by the PX. Handing us each a push broom, they inform us that our mission is to sweep the streets and get rid of the mud puddles. This is the Army Air Corps' idea of a punishment. Of course, there's no way I can let us do this without goofing-off. "Hey guys," I whisper, "follow what I do!"

I start to dance like a fairy as I push the broom up and down the street while prancing through the mud puddles. Abie and Sol join me, and we spin around and around and back through the puddles. Now we have an audience who is laughing and clapping their hands, so we really lay it on. The next puddle is a big one and together we do a flying formation with brooms up in the air, with Sol on my right and Abie on my left. We circle the puddle and set the brooms down on the ground, then pirouette through it while the crowd cheers wildly. The MPs arrive shortly and without further ado, load us onto a truck and bring us back to our barracks to await our next punishment.

After evening chow we are resting on our sacks minding our own business, when an orderly comes through. "Shipping orders are posted on the bulletin board."

We all run to check the list, jostling each other to get to the front. When we finally manage to get to the board, we note that the three "privates" are first on the list to be shipped out. We are going to Ardmore, Oklahoma to be assigned to a crew of ten men on a B-17 for crew training. Lemmon, Foster and I hug. We did it!

CREW TRAINING
Ardmore, Oklahoma
April to June 1944

A few days later we arrive in Ardmore. We are met by a sergeant who has us fall into formation. "Holbrook. Lemmon. Foster. Fall out."

He looks us over and shakes his head. "Get in the jeep. You birds are to report to headquarters." We are driven to the airbase outside of Ardmore. At headquarters, we are met by a captain who leads us to his desk.

"Sit down, men. I see by your orders that your M.O.S. (Military Operation Specialty) is 611. What the hell does that mean?"

"It means, sir, we are the first class to graduate as M.O.S. 611 Carrier Gunners."

"Holbrook, Foster, I see you are tail gunners, and Lemmon, I see you are a ball turret gunner. How the hell do you guys you fit into your positions? Holbrook, it says here that you're six foot tall and weigh 186 pounds. Lemmon, it says you're 5'11" and weigh 160. And Foster, you're 5'10" and weigh 170. It must be a hell of a squeeze!"

And I see that you men were PFCs for five days and then were reduced to privates. In order for you to be assigned to a crew, you have to be at least a corporal. So I guess I promote you to corporal. And you each get ten dollars a month for hazard pay." He assigns Foster and Lemmon each to a crew and then turns to me.

"Don Wood's crew needs a tail gunner. Holbrook, you're assigned to his crew. You take off in thirty minutes. It's his turn for practice today."

He hands us each our corporal stripes and a payroll book. "How you three stuck together is beyond me. Good luck men, we need more like you!"

My buddy, Filz and I

I go out the door with my gear to a jeep that runs me down to the flight line. We pull up by an old B-17F. One of the crew holds the door open and I crawl in with my gear. I sit down and the other guys give me the "hi" sign as we go down the runway.

We climb up to 7000 feet and level off. I introduce myself as 611 Tail Gunner Holbrook. They introduce themselves.

"611 Merril Filz, Ball Turret Gunner."

"611 Howard Hoyt, Waist Gunner."

"611 Robert Foote, Waist Gunner."

They laugh. We all know about you, Holbrook. You were the first ones listed on the shipping orders, *Private*. We liked the shit-eating grin you had on your face when the captain pulled off your stripes."

We circle the field and come in for a landing and taxi to park the B-17. The crew up front comes back through the radio room and introduce themselves.

"Bob Flanagan, Co-Pilot"

"Gus Kroschewsky, Bombardier."

"Tom Reinhardt, Navigator."

"Warren Brown, Crew Chief."

"Norman Ashe, Radio Operator."

"Don Wood, Pilot"

I have now met all of the members of our ten-man crew.

I turned to Wood. "Beautiful landing. I thought B-17s always bounced three times when they came in to land?"

"You must have taken your training at Vegas," he said. "That's where copilots do their first landing, while you gunners ride along."

He filled us in a little bit on the base. "For your information, this base is built on Gene Autrey's 8000 acre ranch. We can bomb targets before the hills and we will be flying over the Gulf where you gunners can shoot at targets in the water. Make sure to read the bulletin board for more information."

A G.I. truck picks us up and takes us to our barracks. I am told that this camp is a copy of the airbase in Norwich, England. This is so the crews that go to England know what their base looks like when they are flying over it. The streets even have the same names. A sign by our front door says 'Norwich Stragglers die'. Nice greeting. We go in, pick out a bunk and unpack our gear.

As I sit down, I hear a voice hollering, "Holbrook!" It's Lemmon, and Foster's with him, so I join them and off we go to the chow hall. I'm glad we're back together again.

We don't fly the next day, so we get class A passes and hop on the bus that goes into Ardmore. Earlier, when I was in the air, I saw that the only tall building in town was the Hotel Ardmore. The crew chief told me to go to the Glider Room, a haven for disillusioned gunners such as myself.

Once we arrive we look around. We can see the whole town in a glance. It is a small town with a narrow main street and train tracks running through the center of town. We leave the bus stop and head for the closest tavern. When we walk in the door, Gene Autrey is singing on the jukebox, and sitting around the table playing Dominos are some tough-looking cowboys.

"I thought cowboys always played poker," I tell the bartender.

He smiles. "This is Gene's town and you are on his land. We haven't had a shootout in years." He serves us our beer.

After a couple of beers, we drink up and set off to find the Glider Room in the Hotel Ardmore. We don't have far to go. The Hotel Ardmore is a large, rambling building on the main street. The waiter greets us and says, "Oklahoma is dry gents, so if you want a bottle of old horse piss, I will serve you with a set up for $4.75. Other that that, it's bottled beer."

We'd already had beer, so we decide to go with the horse piss and Cola for a wash. "Set us up, bartender!"

When the fifth is about half gone, I tell the guys I have looked at the maps and that Dallas is only about 90 miles from here. "I don't fly tomorrow, so I'm checking the bus schedule to see if I can get to where good times can be had."

About that time the waiter ambles up. "Men, drink up! It's 10:30 and they have a curfew around here. All G.I.s and dogs have to be off the street by 11 p.m." We didn't leave him a tip. We catch the bus and as we head back to camp we belt out our favorite tune, *We Are the Best Damn Gunners Yet.*

I have a class at 1000 hours to learn all about the tail gunner position. We are in the classroom waiting for the instructor when he rushes in late and all out of breath. It seems a B-17 with a full crew was flying over a golf course when the pilot decided to buzz it. He banked more than 30 degrees, fell off, and plowed into the ground.

"Who here can drive a truck?" he asks. I told him that I could, so we head over to the motor pool to pick up the truck and head out to the golf course.

On the way he tells me, "If the tail is lying by itself, we can bring it back and set it up in the class room." He is excited as we start up the driveway that overlooks the golf course. I stop the truck and we look at the crash site. Parts of the B-17 are scattered everywhere and the tail is obviously a complete wreck.

"Instructor, I suggest we get the hell out of here before they put us on body bag detail and we find ourselves picking up remains of the crew. Then they'll send us to the cemetery at Jefferson Barracks in St. Louis for the crash victim's burial." He is in complete agreement, so with a couple of quick turns of the steering wheel, we are out of there and driving back to base.

Later on I go to see my pilot to get a pass to visit Dallas for the weekend. The first thing I do is pull out my low cut dancing shoes. They still have a nice shine. At 1800 hours I take the bus to Dallas, which is 90 miles from Ardmore. I get off the bus and check my suitcase in a bus locker. In my opinion, to see a town right, you've got to walk the streets. So that is what I do.

Dallas is a big city and I mosey on toward downtown. I walk past this nice, big house with a beautiful green lawn. I stand and look at it. I walk across the lawn to get a closer look and run into a sign that says "G.I.s and dogs, keep off the grass!"

I go into the nearest club. Upstairs there is a bouncer that welcomes me. "What's a nice guy like you doing in town?" he asks as he pats me on the back.

There is no place to sit, so I belly up to the bar next to where the waitress picks up the drinks to bring to the tables. It's so good to drink some good beer for a change. After three or four beers, this one waitress seems to like me, so I put my arm around her every time she comes back from waiting on a table. We have fun and laugh a lot, but I must have been keeping her from her job because the bouncer comes over and taps me on the shoulder.

"I think you should go," he says with a smile on his face. "I don't want to have throw you out and watch you bounce down that long set of stairs." So I drink up.

As I am getting ready to leave, the waitress puts down her tray and gives me a big kiss. All the couples at the nearby table give us a big hand as the bouncer walks me to the door. Laughing, I go down the stairs and out on the sidewalk to see more of the town. I'm having lots of fun.

John by his B-17

As I walk about the city, I pass by the Elk's Club. On the marquee board out front, it shows a picture of a band playing and people ballroom dancing. I hear music coming from inside. This is for me! I walk in and stand by the dance floor and look around.

A gentleman gets up from his table and greets me. "Welcome," he says, "I am Mr. Gormann." He seems to be about 50 years old. He promptly introduces me to his companions. "These are my secretaries, Shirley and Charlotte." He has a bottle of whiskey and pours me a drink.

"You look like you love this type of music," he says and encourages me to dance with the girls. After four dances, three drinks, and a whole lot of fun, I plead exhaustion. I tell them I have to find a motel and hit the sack as it is two a.m. As soon as my head hits the pillow I am fast asleep.

The next morning, I wake up just in time to catch the bus back to Ardmore. The guys tell me that I missed all the excitement. One of the crews coming back from the target range dropped a black powder bomb on the railroad tracks dead center in Ardmore. The natives are up in arms! It seems that the crew didn't check the bomb bay, so they didn't notice that one of the powder bombs was hung up on a hanger. When they were making a practice run over the city, the bombardier hit the switch and the bomb was dislodged, covering half of Ardmore with a fine mist of black powder.

The next day, after coming in off a flight, I head with my gear to my bunk in the barracks. I can't believe my eyes! Here is my brother, Donald, asleep in my sack. When I wake him, he jumps up and we hug each other.

Donald is also now in the Air Corps. Because he turned 18 when he was a senior, he got his draft notice while still in school. If he waited to go in after graduation he would be drafted as a foot soldier. Like me, this was a fate he wished to avoid, so he left school early and enlisted in the Air Corps. He has just finished up basic training and is now on his way to

Victorville, California, for more mechanic's training.

I tell him I had gotten a letter from our brother, Dave. Dave's draft status was changed and he has also been drafted. He is in basic training and is now stationed at Camp Hood in Texas, which is 60 miles south of Dallas. "He said his beer belly is shrinking from physical training and running with a pack on his back and a M1 Gerand in his hand." In the letter he included a money order for fifteen dollars, so I figured we could go into town for supper. I tell Don that now is a good time to use it.

"I want you to meet my two buddies, Abie and Sol," I tell him. We pick them up on the way to the bus and then we all go to a restaurant I know, where we can get a good t-bone steak and a bottle of beer for $1.25. The steak meets all our expectations and fills us up. We all sit around shooting the bull after supper.

Lemmon asks Don, "How does your brother always come up with a twenty dollar bill? We're always broke by pay day! Watch," he predicted, "he'll pick up the tab." I pick up the bill and pay on the way out. We are off to the Glider room at the Hotel Ardmore.

When we arrive the waiter takes us to a table. "You guys look like you're up to no good," he says. I asked him to bring us the best fifth in the bar with a set up. We have a great time with lots of laughter. When 1100 hours roll around it is time to put Don on the train for California. As we bid him goodbye I wonder when, or if, I will see him again. It is June 10, 1944.

The next day we fly down over the Gulf of Mexico where there are targets floating on the water. The targets give the navigators a heading to follow and something for the gunners to shoot at. The radio gunner receives a call from base instructing us to head for Galveston. Tornados are going through Oklahoma and are headed towards us. We land in late afternoon and spend the night there.

The next morning, as we fly back to Ardmore, we have a bird's eye view of the tornado path. The tornado has cut a swath about a quarter mile wide and ten miles long, zigzagging through the countryside, knocking down oil rigs and ripping roofs off barns. We see a couple of farmhouses that have been flattened, but the tornado has missed the city of Ardmore—barely. The base is in good shape when we land.

The next day is our last day of crew training. Wood takes us up to an altitude of 25,000 feet. There are big, fluffy cumulus clouds that make a nice base to land on and float high above the ground. As Wood lands on the clouds, Bob, our copilot, calls back to the tail, "It's your turn, Holbrook. How would you like to take over Wood's controls? " Of course that's a go with me. I take a walk around the bottle of oxygen and make my way toward the cockpit.

I take Wood's place and he goes down in the nose. I get a feel of the controls. "Just in case one of us gets wounded in combat, you can help bring us in for a landing," Wood tells me. On the downwind leg of the approach, I make a twenty-degree bank and line up the plane to land on the top of a cloud. Bob lowers the landing gear and cuts the engines; I set it down so the wheels are just touching the cloud. Then, we pull up as we throttle up to 25,000 RPMs.

Just then, the radio operator gets a message on the intercom. "It's time to head back to the base, boys. You need to start packing your bags. You're shipping out." He tells us that we are first going to Nebraska because they are flying in ten B-17s. When we arrive, each crew will get their plane ready, and in three days time, we will be heading overseas.

P REPARING FOR OVERSEAS
Kearney Air Base, Nebraska
June 1944

A transporter picks us up and we land in Kearney, Nebraska at sundown. G.I. trucks pick us up and dump us off at the barracks. It is June 12, 1944.

The next day we are up at 0600 hours. Briefing is at 0800 hours. At the meeting, a lieutenant tells us we have a lot to do before we are ready to take off for overseas. The engines will have to be run in, guns cleaned, turrets checked out, and more. He has a checklist for each one of us. We are assigned to plane B-17-44-6329, so out to the flight line we go.

The other guys head for the waist door but I go around to the tail. I can't believe my eyes! Here is a half turret with twin-fifties sticking out! I open the escape hatch and crawl in. The position is the same as in the old B-17; you sit down on the little bicycle seat with your legs in a sitting position with the twin-fifties between your knees. There is more head room with a new type of sight. It looks much better than the old B-17s. I crawl pass the tail well and up to the waist. They have to clean the Cosmoline off their guns. The guys up front have their work cut out for them.

I can stand up straight and my head doesn't hit the ceiling, which is surprising. The rest of the crew gives me all the little jobs, like turning in the sheepskins for some heated suits that plug into an outlet to help them stay warm. I draw out ten new parachutes that snap onto our chest harnesses. I wrap my jacket in a seat cushion and store it in a space next to the tail well.

While I'm working, I'm thinking about this WAC I know, Shorty. I had made a date with her earlier in the day. I thought I might need to have her get me some favors when packing for overseas, so I asked her out for a movie. "I would just like someone to talk to," I told her. She agreed to the date and told me she'd meet me at the PX at 1800 hours.

It's finally time to go back to the barracks to get ready for my date. The first thing I have to do is sew my nice, new corporal stripes onto my uniform shirt and pin on my gunner's wings. I put on the shirt to see how I look in the mirror. I have on my new GI pants and my low cut dancing shoes. They still have a nice shine. I'm off to the PX.

Shorty is sitting at a table, so I sit down beside her. Her other nickname is Happy. Over a couple of beers I ask her, "What's your last name?"

"I have an old Indian name – Waters."

I tell her I was raised on a farm near Winooski, Wisconsin. "In your native language, Winooski means Onion. The river running through Winooski is the Onion River." I go on to tell her how I used to swim in the river and about Elkhart Lake on the Quit Qui Oc River, just north of Winooski. We talk about our families and how there were all boys in my family, so I don't know much about girls.   We left to go to the movies.

The movie is a cowboy and Indian flick. The movie ends as the girl is kissing the cowboy. I say to Happy, "Isn't that a nice ending." I walk her back to the WAC unit and I say goodnight to her. "I'll see your tomorrow!" she says, and jumps up to give me a big kiss goodnight.

The next day I get a pass to go into town to a hardware store. I need a pair of adjustable 8" pliers and an 8" screwdriver. I also need some bird shot for my 45 caliber pistol so that I can stagger the clip with one slug and then one bird shot, until the clip is full. This is so if I get shot down and I bail out and land in a wooded area, I can hit either large or small game.

Happy says she can get me a Coleman camp stove with three cans of gas. I get back to the base and head to the tail of the plane. I pack my purchases in the space by the tail well, where I had earlier stored my jacket.

Now it is time to load the fifty-caliber machine guns, along with the shells. Everything checks out good and we are ready for a test flight.

After supper, we are to meet in the briefing room, which has a little stage and ten rows of ten seats, just like a theater. My job is to pick up ten 45 caliber pistols with belts and bring them to the briefing.

Happy sees me and walks along with me to the briefing room. The lieutenant sees me and tells me I'm late. "We're waiting to start the meeting."

Just then Happy jumps up into my arms and give me a great big kiss. To my horror, in the door come her two buddies. One kisses me on the forehead and the other kisses me on my cheek.

A voice from the podium says, "Wood, where is your tail Gunner?"

Down the isle I go with my hair all messed up and big, red kiss marks all over my face. The guys all whistle and applaud. I sit down with a bow. The lieutenant says, "It looks like this cowboy is ready to ride out into the sunset with the rest of you. Your first stop is Bangor, Maine."

G OING OVERSEAS
June 1944

I am an Army Air Corps tail gunner on a ten-man crew aboard a B-17 airplane. I am part of the Don C. Wood's Crew of the 817th Squadron of the 483rd Bomb Group. I'm headed overseas for my first combat mission. It is July 13, 1944.

We take off at sunset, and as we pass over Wisconsin, I can just make out the line of Lake Michigan. The lights twinkle out as we fly over, as if there is a drill to see what would happen if we had an air raid. I snap open a can of beer and hold it up high in salute to all my friends in Wisconsin. "Prost!" I cheer, as we fly over my home state and beyond to a new horizon.

We arrive in Bangor early the next morning. After some quick shut-eye and chow we are back in the plane. We leave Bangor as the sun is setting in the west, circling the field at an altitude of 8,000 feet. We are headed to Grenier Field, New Hampshire for a rest and fuel stop before continuing on our journey overseas.

The sun is just coming up as we approach Grenier Field and we sail in for a landing. The rest of the crew head for the sack, but I am wound up, as I slept on the plane.

The gas tankard pulls alongside the plane as I hop onto the wing. I pop the gas cap and put the nozzle into the gas tank. I let my gaze wander along the street that runs along the main gate and immediately my eyes land on a long, red Miller High Life sign. I hop down off the wing and crawl up into the cab to shoot the bull with the driver for a few minutes. I lament that I haven't had a Miller since I left Milwaukee. It turns out that he is from Milwaukee, so we have lots of things to talk about. "After we get this baby filled, I will go get you a crewman's pass so you can go have a beer on me," he offers.

After the B-17 is filled with gas he takes off and returns about thirty minutes later with the promised pass. It's like old home week as I walk under that long, red sign. Two High Life's slide down fast and I tell the bartender to set out a six-pack to go. That is all I have room for in the tail. I head back to the plane and settle down with my beer.

After six hours, the crew is back and they pile into the plane. My job is to stand underneath the engines with a fire extinguisher as the engine turns over slowly and spurts. If there is a fire I am ready to put it out. The engines start up one at a time and when all four engines are running smoothly, I crawl into the waist, store the extinguisher, and pull the door shut. We are off down the runway.

We fly over Canada at dusk so I can barely see the beautiful lakes and trees that I know are there. We fly all night and as the sun is just starting to peak on the horizon, we land for another rest and fuel stop at the Air Base in Newfoundland. Brother, it is cold up here! We are very happy that they have steam-heated barracks. After a hearty breakfast we all hit the sack and sleep for six hours.

When we are woken up, we are taken to the briefing room. The captain briefs us about the upcoming weather and hands the navigator a letter with our sealed orders. The words, GANDER, NEWFOUNDLAND, are carefully inscribed on the outside of the envelope. He instructs us to open the envelope when we have circled the field and cautions us that we must have radio silence so the enemy can not pick up any information. We stare at the envelope that contains our destination and landing instructions, and wonder what is in store for us.

It gets dark early up here and we feel the cold blasts of wind through our jackets. The props pull easily with three of us pulling on them.

We have a small auxiliary generator, called a Putt Putt, which is on skids.
We pull it out of the waist door and I plug it into the first engine so we have
enough power to turn the engine over. It spurts and starts running with a
hum. The other three start up smoothly, too. We push the putt-putt back
to the waist door and push it through. I go get the fire extinguisher that
was standing by in case of fire and secure it inside the plane. I close the
door as we take off down the runway.

     I am in the radio room with Reinhardt. At 8,000 feet he opens the
envelope. As he opens our orders he tells me he thinks we are headed for
England. He is surprised that we are headed to the Azore Islands instead.
Over the intercom, he informs everyone of our destination.

     To me he says, "Where the hell is that?" I tell him that the Azores
are off the coasts of Spain and Africa. He locates the English Channel and
I tell him to find El Aquinas, because it is the largest of the Azore Islands.
I am right on. I get up from the radio room and make my way to the rear
of the plane. I crawl upon the U-four bags in the bomb bay and go to
sleep.

     I wake up to hear Ashe cussing on the radio. He is trying to make
contact with the airfield so we can land. Instead, we hear Germans tell us
that they are going to shoot us down and we won't have a chance to go back
to the U.S.A. They jam up our radio frequency so we have no radio contact
with the base. We are very nervous as this is our first encounter with the
enemy, but we all remain calm. Reinhardt tells us he can see the base just
ahead of us. Wood instructs us to shoot off the distress flares immediately,
as we don't have enough fuel to circle around again and that we have to land
now. As we make the final approach, a flare shoots up from the ground to
let us know we are approved to land. Wood brings us in for a beautiful
landing.

     We pile out and head for the mess hall for some chow. After our bellies are full, the rest of the crew head to the barracks to hit the sack. I slept on the plane, so I return to the plane to guard it to make sure no one takes anything.

I just get back to the plane when the tanker truck pulls up to refuel. The driver hops down from the cab and I help him pull out the big hose. I crawl up on the wing and put the big nozzle into the fuel pipe. As I climb down he asks, "Do you have any blue seal money on you?"

I'm not sure what blue seal money is; he explains that American money has either a blue seal or a green seal on it. The ones with blue seals are worth ten to one on the Islands. I look in my wallet and find both.

"Here's what you do," he says. "See that path that goes straight up the highest hill? Follow the path up this side of the hill and down the other side. At the bottom, there is an old man sitting by the mouth of a cave. You hand him two blue seal dollars and he will go into the cave and come out with two bottles of champagne. It's the best stuff you will ever drink."

I'm always up for an adventure, so with his promise to keep an eye on the plane, I climb up the hill and down the other side. Just as he said, there is an old man at the entrance to the cave. I gave him my two blue seal dollars and he immediately disappears inside. I wait. He returns with two full quart bottles of champagne.

I head back to the landing strip, and as I approach the top of the hill, a low hanging cloud passes and sets down on me. I am standing there thinking, "This is what I always pictured in the bible when Jesus always went to pray." It seems a good time and place to say my own prayer. "O Lord, I'm going to need all the help I can get. Thank you for seeing me this far. Please watch over me and keep me safe."

I continue down the hill and return to the airfield, where the motor is running and the B-17s tanks are still being filled. I hand one of the bottles up to the driver in the cab, and by the time I go around to the other side and crawl up onto the seat, he has popped the cork. Champagne gushes into the air. He takes a big swig and passes the bottle to me. He is right; it is the best champagne I have ever had! We have half of the bottle gone by the time the plane tanks are filled. He tells me to keep the other bottle safely tucked away so it doesn't pop open, and when the time is right, me and my buddies can have one on him.

I meet up with the rest of the guys for chow. Afterwards we go to the orderly room for briefing. We are greeted by a captain who hands us each a backpack. As he passes them around he explains. "You are headed for Marrakech, Africa. You will be flying over the jungle, so you will need these in case you go down. They are jungle survival kits, so in addition to normal survival gear, your back pack includes a machete, fishing line and lures, mosquito repellant, and other items necessary for jungle survival." He shows us how the back packs fit onto the straps of our parachute.

Wood is handed all the paperwork and we return to the plane for take off. It is a straight heading into the middle of Africa. We fly all night and when the sun just peeks over the horizon we sight the air base in Marrakech and come in for a landing. We taxi up to a spot at the edge of the trees and shut down the engines. We are hungry and gladly head to chow.

We are standing in chow line when a medic comes up and tells me to open my mouth. He puts a pill on my tongue. When I ask what it is for, he tells me, "Malaria. I assume you have been taking these for the last two weeks, before leaving the states." When I tell him no, he just shakes his head and walks away.

Once again our bellies are full. I go back to the plane as the rest of the crew head for the sack. I stand under the plane's wing so I am out of the heat of the sun. All of a sudden, four little black fellows come out from the underbrush. They beg for something to eat, so I go to the tail and pull out a bag of Kraft caramels. They watch attentively as I show them how to unwrap the candies. I put some in each little hand and they quickly run off, disappearing back into the underbrush.

Later, as we take off from Marrakech, we fly low over the dessert, heading for Tunisia. I watch the camel caravans as they go from oasis to oasis and am thankful that I don't have to ride along with them on their hot and dusty journey. When we land, we are greeted by Red Cross volunteers who are passing out doughnuts and coffee. They give me a little book with a picture of Sad Sack on the cover that says "Welcome to Tunis." We stay overnight and the next morning we are off again.

As we fly over the Mediterranean, we see Navy battleships sailing across the sea. The ship sends up two good bursts of flak. Tom gets out the blinker, looks up the code of the day, and flashes a code that lets them know we are one of the good guys. I'm glad he's good at that. We sure have a great crew!

We arrive at our final destination, Sterparone Air Base in Italy, on July 19, 1944, just in time to replace the recent German airdrome losses. Fourteen of the group's bombers were lost on the bomb run, while the remaining twelve attacked and destroyed the target, returning safely to base. Fifty-three enemy fighters were destroyed.

We are met at the plane by a little truck and we all throw our gear in the back. The truck takes us to Tent City, where there are thousands of little white tents. They are clearing out the crew gear from the bombers that were shot down. It was piled carelessly outside one of the tents, off to the side, to make room for our gear. The driver tells us to take the tent we want and drives off, bidding us a good day.

We pick the first one and begin to stow our gear. I look at the cot and don't see any blankets, so I go out to the pile and pick up two G.I. blankets to put down on my cot to sleep on. How lovely! And we thought we were going to England. I go back out and pick out a packing crate with three little shelves that the former guy had. I also spy a little table, so with someplace to put my stuff, I begin to unpack.

I put my Coleman, a frying pan and a box of 45 caliber slugs on the bottom shelf of the crate. I carefully place Ethel's picture on the second shelf so I can look at it before I go to sleep and when I wake up. The top is reserved for my nicely shined low-cut dancing shoes. I set the table off to the side. The rest of the crew has stored their gear, too. We look around. Home Sweet Home.

We go down the grade to the mess tent. Behind the tent is a stockade with Italian and German prisoners. They can tell a new crew when they see one and they taunt us in broken English, "You're going to get shot down!" I give them the old salute– left hand under the elbow with the right arm straight up, fist clenched. I get a rousing response.

We go through the chow line. The cooks are busy rehydrating food and opening cans. The tea is in a garbage can on top of a burner, boiling away. They have good baked bread, with the finest butter. The coffee is good, hot and strong and the dehydrated potatoes are not so bad either.

Brown tells Ashe: "We need a radio so we can pick up Axis Sally's music." He hands him a piece of paper with a list of supplies. "If you can get me one tube and these parts, I can put together a set that will bring in the German Messingers.

Hoyt always carries a piece of chalk in his pocket. He disappears out through the tent flap and we can see his shadow along the side of the tent, bobbing up and down. We all go out to look at what he's up to. On the side of the tent he has scrawled in big letters: *ELEANOR HATES WAR – FALA DOES TOO!*

C OMBAT DUTY
Sterparone Air Base, Genoa, Italy
July to November 1944

We meet with Colonel Sperry and his staff at 0900 hours. I've now been in this man's army for 7 months, 13 days, and am now being briefed on my first combat mission. He tells us that we are about to fly on a very important mission. We are to hit a chemical plant and oil refinery at Brux, Czechoslovakia, just east of Vienna. Our mission will be to take out or cripple the flow of oil to the enemy, while at the same time, the 8th air force will be hitting the chemical factory outside of Berlin. Lieutenant Black will fly copilot because we are a first-time crew.

"The German's have changed the pursuit curve to a higher elevation. They come straight down and shoot up the tail gunners. Then an ME 210, with a canon in its nose, will try to come in and blow the tail off the plane. If that happens, you go down."

He looks at me. "Corporal Holbrook, you are now a staff sergeant. If you bail out and land in enemy territory, the Germans are less likely to shoot you so fast if you carry some rank. Here are your stripes. Get them sewn on before tomorrow."

"We will go with two Squads. Wood, you and your crew will be assigned to the 817th Squad. Your crew is to be in their positions on take off with the ball turret gunner standing by the ball. We are about 60 miles from front lines and fighters might jump you on take off, so be careful. H-Hour will be at 0530. Take off will be at 0730. Dismissed!"

I lay in my bed until late at night, wondering what my first mission will be like. I want to remember what happens and how it feels to be part of this war, so I decide I am going to try and write down information about my missions to help me remember later. I miss my girl, Ethel, and wonder if I will get to hold her in my arms again.

Journal Entry: 21 July

    H-Hour: 0530 hours.

    Takeoff: 0730 hours.

    Target: The chemical plant and oil refinery in Brux, Czechoslovakia.

    We hear the sound of a horn and we are up. The sun is just peaking through the skyline. I slept with all my clothes on so that I can be the first one out to the shit trench. I pull down my pants and back up to it. There is a shovel sticking in the loose earth so I cover up my deposit. I head off to chow and am glad I am up early, because the chow line is still short.

    At 0630 hours, a small truck picks us up by our tent and takes us down to the flight line. It is a very dusty ride, for this was once a wheat field. The crew separates and go to their positions. I open the escape door to the tail and I sit in the opening as I pull on my coveralls that cover my 45 caliber pistol. It is loaded with one bird shot and one slug. I pull up my pants leg and strap a French knife to my leg just below my knee. Over this I put on my heated suit. On goes my seat pack parachutes with the harness for my chest pack chute, which I set just past the door by the tail wheel. I like having a spare in case one gets a hole in it. I crawl into position and it's a tight squeeze. When I'm finally in I pull the door shut and crawl on my knees over a bicycle seat that is bolted to the floor.

    I'm on my knees with my feet spread out side ways. I check the guns and check the gauge on the oxygen tank. I plug in my ear phones and mic. Because Black is flying copilot, Flannigan's not with us today. I'm going to miss him as he is always looking out for me in the tail. Ashe runs the check and the entire crew is ready to go.

    We taxi down to the end of the runway and wait for the plane in front of us to take off. Woods taxies into position and the ground crew give us the go signal. We race down the matted runway and the front of the ship lifts into the air. I look around at the tail wheel and it is bobbing up and down. I hope it doesn't come loose, because if it does, I will be nothing but a grease spot on the runway.

We are off. We circle the base to gain altitude and at the same time we are forming our squad. Three of our B-17s form a V, almost touching wing tips, and just below us are three more B-17s, also in a V formation with their wings almost touching. Below them is one more B-17, called the tail-end Charlie. We then pull up to a second squad and together, we are on our way to Brux.

We have an escort of P-38s that meet us over the Adriatic Sea. We

Headquarters at Sterperone Air Base
This is where the big brass sleeps and work,
and where the service club, mess hall
and church are located.

fly over the Alps and into Austria where we are quickly attacked by ME 109s. As predicted, they come at us, straight down from about a 40,000 foot altitude. The upper turret gunners blast away when one goes past our tail, and pulls up. I send some more bullets flying at him. He is met with a P-38 that finishes him off. I watch the dog fights and see one P-38 go down in flames.

Our escort leaves us as we are flying over Austria. I'm starting to get nervous; this is going to be hell without an escort. Our target is in the northern part of Czechoslovakia. The other squad veers off towards the chemical factory while we head towards the oil refinery. The flak is bursting all around us as the bomb bay doors are opened. Gus sounds off, "Bomb's Away!" The ship lifts up from the weight that has been released.

Black takes evasive action as we regroup and head for home. Wood comes on the intercom to report that we have lost three B-17s. "How is everything in the tail?"

Brown reports he sees lots of little holes. I tell him I am okay, but there is a little breeze going past me and out the link short. All in all, we are in good shape. We are lucky to pick up a tail wind going back to base so the trip back is a little shorter than the trip there.

We come in for a landing that is sensational, as all of a sudden, the tail taps on the matted runway. We taxi to the hardstand. I slowly get up from my knees and try to gain my sea legs. As I reach for the door lock, the door opens and we are greeted by our ground crew chief.

"Thank heavens you're okay. I heard over the squawk box that a tail gunner was strafed and died over his twin fifties. I'm sure glad you made it back safely." He introduces himself, but I can't hear him well over the noise. I did, however, hear him say he is from Arkansas.

I introduce myself as Hyman from Wisconsin. "Mind if I call you R'key?" We chat for awhile before we pile on the truck. We are dropped at headquarters, where we are briefed about the mission. The lieutenant passes out whiskey glasses and pours us each a shot to celebrate a safe return from our first mission. We quickly debrief him and are off to chow. By the time we walk back to our tent we are dead tired. We stop at the bulletin board to check out tomorrow's mission. We are to take off at 0720 hours for the Ploesti Oil Fields in Romania.

Now that I have been on one mission, I wonder how the hell I am going to make it through 50! I am told that the 483rd gets sent to targets that are the most heavily defended in Europe: major oil refineries, aircraft and parts factories, tank works, railroad terminals and hauling yards, supply dumps, bridges and communication networks.. I hope I live to tell about it!

Plane on matted runway

Journal Entry: 22 July

We take off as scheduled at 0720 hours. We are expected to be over the oil fields by 1100 hours. Today we have an escort of P-51s as we fly over the Adriatic Sea. They continue to follow us inland where they have to turn around and fly back to Italy, as they only have enough fuel to go this far and back to their base.

At 1030 hours, the squad behind us is attacked by ME-210 German fighters. As I watch, I see two B-17s spiral down in flames. Gus calls out and the bomb bay doors are opened. The flak is so thick I don't know how we are able to fly through it without getting a direct hit on the plane. He

Bomb strike photo

calls out, "bombs away", and we drop our load. As we turn and head for home I can see the exploding oil tanks and buildings on fire. The smoke comes up to the low cumulous clouds below us. It was a good hit.

It has been a long mission—nine hours. The tower tells us there are bad winds and directs us to a P-38 airfield south of Foggia, where we will spend the night.

Journal Entry: 23 July

We fly back to Sterparone Air Base and arrive just in time for chow. Later, as we are stretched out on our cots and relaxing in our tent, a little Italian boy enters through the doorway and announces, "I'm Tony. I do many things. I take laundry to town. I have fresh eggs."

Tony spies my nicely shined shoes. "I can get forty dollars for shoes from uncle in Foggia. He has a nice big house that is across from Red Cross. You follow path that leads over to bombed-out railroad tracks. He gives you vino in the green bottle and fresh cakes made from barley, all for forty dollars. Good deal."

I tell him: "No thanks Tony. But you can help me. See this cup? See how I put one lira under it? You check every day, and when you see there is a lira under the cup, you take the money and leave me an egg."

I can get bread from the chow line and my Uncle Erick sends me cheese every two weeks, so I can have a sandwich before I hit the sack. With my burner and frying pan, I will now be able to enjoy a fresh egg for breakfast. All the comforts of home!

Journal Entry: 24 July

I find an article in the military newspaper about yesterday's mission. I decide I'm going to try to find and cut out articles about the missions we go on. This is the first one.

Exert from Stars & Strips: Ploesti Again 15th Target: 23 July

MAAF HEADQUARTERS—Strong forces on 15th Air Force heavy bombers ranged over Romania yesterday to give the Romania Americana oil refinery at Ploesti another blasting and smash again at the Iron Gate bridge and rail yards and Eraljevo bridge.

Meanwhile, tactical aircraft struck at objectives in northwest Italy and along the east coast of the peninsula.

A smoke screen hampered observation at Ploesti, but a spiral of black smoke 15,000 feet high was seen and photos showed fresh hits on storage facilities. Oil fires were visible at Unirea Spiranza in the same area. Fortresses achieved good results at the Iron Gate. Liberators pounded the Doagujeyak railroad yards.

Thunderbolts pounded communications in the Pisa region while

Cameras mounted on the waist gun
automatically take photos.
This is a picture of one of the planes
in our squadron going down.

fighter bombers were active over the battle area despite bad weather. A bridge, quay and the harbor side at Pesaro, on the east coast, were hit and other strikes were reported on the Ravenna rail yards.

Journal Entry: 25 July

H-Hour: 0430. Takeoff: 0730. Target: Herman Goring Tank Factory and Repair Shop in Linz, Austria.

Flak is heavy. We hit the target and everything explodes into fire. That should help our men on the ground. We caught seven flak holes, one directly above my head.

We made it back safely so I shouldn't complain, but I really could use a shower. Oh yea, we don't have any!

Journal Entry: 26 July

Takeoff: 0800. Target: The ME-109 factory in Weiner Neudorf, Austria. We are escorted by P-51s and P-38s. We make two passes at the target but are unable to drop the bombs. We head toward the alternate target in Vienna and ride through heavy flak, which takes out engine number two and engine number four. Oil hits the slit stream, giving the rest of the plane an oil bath. We lose eleven planes.

Journal Entry: 28 July

H-Hour 0330. Target 11:20. Ploesti, Romania oil fields.

The flak is so heavy I don't know how we can fly through it. They had briefed us for 500 solid gun emplacements. Over the intercom we hear Reinhardt cough. He's been hit in the face mask. Gus has to drop the bombs before he can help him. He yells "bombs away" and turns to Reinhart to help him, but he tells us he's okay. A big piece of flak sails behind me and puts a big hole through the rudder just behind my head.

We take elevation up above the flak and look down. We can tell we really plastered the oil wells by the clouds of smoke high into the air. Woods comes on the intercom to tell us we are 500 miles from our target. We can still see the clouds of smoke. We head back to the base.

Journal Entry: 30 July

Destination: Budapest, Hungary

Budapest is a hot target with oil wells and pipe lines that supply the German army and air force.

Our copilot, Bob Flannigan, is flying with another crew today. As we circle the airfield and get into formation, a B-17 pulls up to our wing. I can see Flannigan. I give him the "Hi" sign and he answers back with a big smile.

. As we come in on the bomb run, the flak bursts are on us, shaking the plane. I look out my window and see Flannigan's plane taking a direct hit that blows the tail off, sending pieces flying past my window. I watch as his plane makes a wide circle going down and disappear under the clouds below us.

Journal Entry: 31 July

H-Hour: 0430. Takeoff: 0700. Target: Ploesti oil fields, Rumania.

We are escorted by P-38s. The flack is very heavy, intense and accurate. As I watch, a B-17 goes down in a ball of fire and I see five parachutes come out. One of the chutes immediately bursts into flames and down it goes.

Our plane has 26 flak holes. We have holes on the wing tip, in the bomb bay, throughout the waist and tail. I see gasoline leaking from the tank in a small but steady little stream. We barely make it back to the base. We come straight into the runway and taxi to the hardstand. The engines have just died down when the door is wrenched open. Sure enough, good old R'key is here to make sure I am okay.

I crawl out and gave him a big hug. I asked him how many days he thinks it will take to patch up the plane. "Take your time!" I say as I head for chow. I am dead tired and can barely make it to the sack after I eat.

Later, when we are lying in our sacks, I ask when we are going to name our plane. "When we sight an enemy plane, Wood always shouts *tally ho*, so I think we should paint a picture of a fox on the side of the plane with the words *Tally Ho*." My idea, however, gets shot down quickly. We never did name the plane.

Excerpt from Stars & Stripes: 1 August

P51 BAGS 30 ENEMY PLANES—Thirty German planes were shot down out of 50 in an aerial battle of mass tactics yesterday when the enemy formation attempted to intercept two squadrons from the veteran 15th AAF Mustang groups, which joined forces for the flight while escorting bombers to the Bucharest oil installations. Only one Mustang was lost.

One unit, part of the 325th Fighter Group, shot down 18 planes to run the group's total to 404 since it began flying in combat 17 April 1943. The other squadron belongs to the 31st Fighter Group which has been in operation since 12 August 1942.

The enemy formation of ME-109s and FW-190s flew in for the attack from the south at well over 30,000 feet. The German pilots formed a tight Lufbery Circle, with each plane protecting another's tail. The tactic was a trap, and the circle was forced down to 8,000 feet, where it disintegrated. The Mustangs scored victories all the way down.

First Lt. Harry A Parker, 28, Grove St., Milford, NH shot down four ME-109s to score his squadron's 100th win and his groups 400th. The victories brought Parker's personal total to eight enemy craft destroyed in the last five days.

"When we spied the Jerries go into a Lufbery Circle, we did the same but on the outside and flying in the opposite direction." Parker said. "I fired at ten planes. Two crashed and two pilots bailed out."

After the battle, the fighters continued on the trip to Bucharest where the bombers dropped their eggs over oil storage depots and installations. Results were described as fair with smoke seen rising to 15,000 feet.

Maj. Gen. Nathan F. Twining, commanding general of the 15th AAF, sent the following message to all units of his command today, in commemoration of the 37th anniversary of the founding of the Army Air

B-17s flying in formation

Force on 1 August 1907.

"No better demonstration of the degree of rightful pride, which all in the 15th Air Force feel on this occasion, can be afforded than by rededicating ourselves to the sole task before us—the speeds and complete defeat of our enemies. In the accomplishment of our present objective, our units have been given the privilege of a unique and enviable role.

"We can nullify the enemy's air power by continuing to strike at his few remaining industrial centers. Our fighter pilots and bomber gunners can exact a high toll of any enemy opposition which may be forthcoming.

"Our enemies are desperate and in desperation there is often hidden strength. No opportunity must be given for them to recover from the blows that are being and will be dealt."

Journal Entry: 2 August

H-Hour: 0330. Take off 0630 Target: the torpedo factory in Portes Les Valence, France

We were called to headquarters yesterday and informed that another crew took our B-17 and ditched it in the Adriatic Sea. (So much for naming our plane.) We will now be using the old model F-F-17. What a low blow! Now I can barely squeeze into position and have absolutely no room to move around. Our other plane had twin fifties that were mounted on a swivel that could move from side to side and up and down, with a sight that followed with the guns.

We set out for Valance with a P-51 Escort. We weren't expecting a lot of resistance, so, as promised, it was a milk run.

Journal Entry: 3 August

Target: A chemical factory in Friedrichshafen, Germany

We are escorted by a P-51. The flak is moderate and we get only a few holes, but the 816th squadron flying to my left is getting heavy flak. I see the tail gun bobbing up and down in one of the B-17s. It's my buddy, Foster. We have a signal worked out where we move our tail guns up and down so we would know what B-17s we are in. I answer back by moving my tail guns up and down.

Their plane has lost two engines and has dropped out of formation. They lose another engine and just manage to make it over the Alps. They

The Don C. Wood's Crew
Front Row
John Holbrook, Merril Filz, Howard Hoyt, Robert Foote
Back Row
Don Jones (who sometimes flew with the crew), Thomas Reinhardt, Dan Wood
At the time of this photo,
Gus Kroschewsky has been killed in action
Warren Brown is in the hospital with appendicitis
Norman Ashe had contracted spinal meningitis and has been sent home
Robert Flannigan's is listed missing in action

are ditching the plane in the Adriatic Sea. With my binoculars, I watch Mullins land the ship. I see one raft come out from the radio room. Ashe has radioed the base so that they can send out a PB-4 to pick up the crew.

We return to the air base and anxiously wait for news. About an hour later the PB-4 comes in with the crew. Lemmon and I run out to greet them and to see how our boy is doing. The crew has bagged up Foster's ear, as it has separated from his head. The medic sews his ear back on and loads the crew into the ambulance and they are off to the hospital on Foggia.

Exert from Stars & Stripes: MAAF Heavies Hit Targets in Silesia: 7 August

MAAF HEADQUARTERS— Germany's dwindling oil supply took another heavy punch today when a medium force of 15th AAF Liberators and Fortress raided two synthetics plants at Blechhammer, 75 miles southeast of Breslau, in Silesia, according to an official communiqué.

Intense flak was reported over both targets, but escorting Mustangs and Lightnings met few intercepting enemy aircraft, the announcement declared. Though one formation of Liberators bombed by instruments the northernmost plant, obscured by a smoke screen, good results were reported at both targets.

The two installations, four miles apart, produced a good share of high grade gas for the German armed forces. The were last attacked by 15th AFF on July 7.

Exert from Stars & Stripes: 8 August

8TH BOMBERS LAND AT 15TH AIRDROMES— Heavy bombers of the 8th AAF which yesterday bombed a German factory in Poland on their way to Russia, today landed at 15th AAF bases after pounding two enemy airdromes in the Ploesti Area of Rumania on the second leg of their triangle-shuttle flight.

All aircraft landed in Russia without loss yesterday after attacking a
Nazi factory at Rahmel, 10 miles northwest of the Polish port of Gdynia.
Few enemy aircraft were encountered, but flak was reported heavy at some
points.

Airdromes in Rumania at Buzau and Zillstea were bombed today
without serious interception, and British based escorting Mustangs reported
one victory over the Lutfwaffe. The attacks were the 20th such operation
since shuttle bombing technique was inaugurated by 15th AAF on June 2.

An announcement today disclosed that 29 enemy aircraft were
destroyed by fighters and bomber gunners participating in yesterday's 15th
AAF raid on two synthetics oil plants at Blechhammer.

Journal Entry: 10 August
H-Hour: 0300. Target: Ploesti Oil Refinery.   The flight in goes smoothly.
Although the flak is intense, good navigation saves us from direct hits. We
are lucky to get only a few flak holes. I watch the oil tanks below and the
smoke climbing closer to us. We can still see it as we head back to the base.

Journal Entry: 13 August
        Target: Coastal Defense in Savona, Italy
        The mission was pretty routine, although some planes were hit by
heavy flak. We get back to the base by 1500 hours. R'key greets me and
asks me to help him load frag bombs. They are tied in bundles and we tie
them to the hooks that release the bombs.

Journal Entry: 14 August
        Target: Toulon, France
        We are in position to provide general invasion support. There is

radio silence. We arrive over the target in late afternoon. The bombardier says, "bombs away". The long, slender bombs have fins that fly in all different directions. The shards make the Germans retreat to the hills.

The 815th and the 840th bomb groups take off again at midnight with 500 pound bombs to hit the hills offshore to dig holes for invasion support. One radio operator reported that they flew over the invasion ships and reported it looks like a sea of steel!

Journal Entry: 16 August

Target: The railroad bridge in Valence, France

Routine mission with no escort. Light flak.

Heavy flak makes flying

Excerpt from Stars and Stripes: 16 August
15TH HEAVIES TO POLESTI TARGETS—Aug. 16—Strong
forces of 15th AAF Liberators and Fortresses for the second time in 24

European Theater of Operation

hours, returned to Ploesti, Rumania, today to pound oil installations there and at Campina, 19 miles to the northwest, according to an official announcement.

A formation of Liberators also blasted the Albunar airdrome in Yugoslavia, near the Rumanian border. All of the heavies were escorted by fighters which carried out offensive sweeps in the target areas where no enemy aircraft appeared to challenge the bombers.

Though a smoke screen hung over the Ploesti objectives, most of the bombing was visual and good results were reported. Flak was intense.

Twenty heavy bombers and four fighters were listed as missing after yesterday's attacks on the Ploesti oil center and the Nis, Yugoslavia, airdrome. Two enemy aircraft destroyed during the raids were credited to Lt. John J. Voll, Cincinnati, who brought his individual score to eights when three ME-109s attacked him as he returned alone after protecting a comrade who parachuted into enemy territory.

Medium and attack bombers yesterday continued to pound at transport and communications.

Journal Entry: 16 August

Target: Oil refinery outside of Germany

The oil refinery is actually in Poland, just east of Brux. It is a long mission. The Russians are on the move and it looks like they will take Ploesti. The Flak is heavy and the enemy has a lot of mobile guns in addition to solid gun emplacements. We came out of the run with some holes in our plane, but it looks like a good strike. Bulls Eye!

Journal Entry: 18 August

Target: Ploesti Oil Refinery

We are escorted by P-51s. It is a rough day. We are hit hard before we reach our target. I have a six pack of beer along, carefully tucked behind me. Flak hits all the cans and I watch it freeze in a puddle. I guess there will be no beer today!

Engine number four takes a direct hit and Wood has to feather it by adjusting the controllable-pitch propeller to a pitch position so the blade angle is about ninety degrees to the plane of rotation. This stops the plane from wind milling. We quickly drop out of formation and stagger back to base, but we make it safely.

Excerpt from Stars & Stripes: 22 August

1,500 ALLIED SHIPS IN RIVIERA LANDING—It didn't show through the flashing roar of the guns of the 1,500 ships and craft operating in the southern France assault forces, but there was plenty of gold braid tucked away in lockers of the warships in the bombardment. No less than ten rear admirals, eight of them American, were on hand to carry out the orders of Vice Admiral H. Kent Hewitt, commanding the naval forced involved.

It was announced today that Rear Admirals Frank J. Lowry, Bertram J. Rodgers and Spencer F. Lewis commanded the three principal naval assault forces. In command of the fleets' gunfire support groups that included battleships, cruisers and destroyers, were Rear Admirals J. H. Mansfield, Royal Vavy Lyal A. Davidson, Carleton F. Bryand, M L. Deyo and Theodore E. Ohandler. In charge of aircraft Carriers were Rear Admirals Thomas Troubridge, Royal Navy, and Calvin T. Durgin.

Of the 1,500 vessels in the operation 641 flew the American flag.

Exert from Stars & Stripes: 22 August

STRONG 15TH FORCES ATTACK ON OIL TARGETS—Strong forces of 15th AAF heavy bombers today attacked synthetic oil objectives in Silesta and natural oil targets near Vienna, encountering a considerable number of enemy aircraft for the first time since August 7.

Hard battles went on in the Vienna-Budapest fighter defense belt between interceptors and Liberators bombing the Austrian oil installations. Gunners and the escorting Mustang and Lightnings scored a number of victories.

Flying Forts and Liberators attacked the northern targets also escorted by Mustangs and Lightenings, reporting only a few encounters. Their objectives were protected by a smoke screen and most groups bombed by instruments.

At the Odertal synthetic refinery, 80 miles southwest of Breslau, some Fort formations reported good bombing by visual methods. The refinery there has a normal capacity of 100,000 tons of oil per year.

Journal Entry: 26 August Target: Viaducts in Barovnica, Yugoslavia

This is supposed to be a milk run. Hoyt wants to see how it is in the tail so we trade positions; he goes to the tail and I take over the waist gunner position. There is just one waist gunner today, me, so I cover both sides. Our altitude is about 17,000 feet.

I pull up the wooden ammo box and sit looking out the window and enjoying the view for most of the way. As we come in on the bomb run, a loud blast underneath us knocks me off the box and I end up flat on the floor. Filz, from the ball turret, came to help, but I am okay. It was luck that the flak went out and we only caught the concussion from the blast. This came from a Molie unit. So much for a milk run!

Exert from Stars & Strips: MAAF Opposition in Balkans Declines: 28 August

MAAF HEADQUARTERS— On the fourth successive day over normally well-defended areas of the Balkans strong formations of escorted

15th AAF heavy bombers today provoked slight enemy fighter opposition as they bombed targets in Rumania, Austria and northern Italy.

Points hit included the Moosblerbaum oil refinery, 22 miles northwest of Vienna, the Szony refinery, 50 miles northwest of Budapest, and the rail yards at Miskolcz, Hungary.

The Avisio viaduct and the Ora Bridge on the Brenner Pass line from northern Italy again were plastered by the heavies. Reconnaissance reports showed that as a result of recent concentrated raids on communication lines into northern Italy, all but one of the railways leading into Germany, Austria and Yugoslavia have been cut. The Brenner Pass line was severed at Avisio.

Journal Entry: 30 August

    H-Hour: 0430. Target Time 1055.

    Target: Hit bridges in Barvica, Yugoslavia.

    Today's mission turns out to be a milk run, which was a good deal after a week's rest. We are now flying in the old model FB-17s. The truth is out that the 90th Bomb Group flies in with old model Fs and takes the new B-17s back to their base. I guess that is what happens when they pull rank over you. They were in Italy before the 483rd.

Journal Entry: 31 August

    The Russians have taken over Rumania. *R'key* comes and gets me to help him drop the ball turret and put boards across the hole. He tells me we have just two days to get our prisoners-of-war. We spend the afternoon removing waist guns and fields-stripping the plane of unnecessary gear so that we have as much room as possible for the POWs.

Journal Entry: 1 September

    Target: The Azony Oil Refinery in Budapest

    The refinery is located fifty miles northwest of Budapest. We get a nice hit. Not many 109s waiting for us to shoot us down. As we come in on the downwind leg we have to go back up and go around again. As we are circling, I wonder how many guys went down over the Ploesti Oil Fields and how many have died. I look out and see two B-17s come straight in. They are loaded with Prisoners of War from Rumania. And I wonder how many prisoner's of war are piling into our B-17s. There must be quite a few as it is supposed to take two day to get them out.

    They are headed to our base to be processed and moved on to Naples, where they will be put on a boat for home. I wish I was going to be there to talk with them about what they went through but by the time I get back from my mission, they will already be gone.

Exert from Stars & Stripes: 1,000 Men Evacuated by Heavies: 1 September
   Over 1,000 jubilant AAF combat crewmen, just evacuated from
Rumania, Thursday and Friday poured out of the bellies of 15th AAF B-17
Flying Fortresses onto a sun-baked Italian airdrome, and immediately were
swept into a whirl of equally excited news photographers, war
correspondents, high-ranking officers and surprised bystanders.
   The crewmen some held prisoners for over a year, swarmed onto
the runways in hordes, dressed in motley uniforms. Some had long beards,
but all apparently were in good health, and unable to find words to express
their relief in once again being on Allied soil.
   Some sported German helmets, German and Rumanian officer
uniforms, long and wicked-looking knives, fancy belts and scarves, colorful
shirts and pants. One sergeant, for some unknown reason, had lugged a
complete German field machine gun throughout his travels. Another was
carrying two unopened cases of German hand grenades.
   Rumanian cigarettes, which they purchased in prison camp
canteens, were thrown to the ground or given to curious soldiers and cases
of American cigarettes were opened and eagerly smoked by the airmen. It
was the first American cigarettes they had smoked in many a month.
   A 15th AAF intelligence officer, handling the interrogation of the
returning men, briefed all on just what was to happen to them now that
they were back in Allied hands. "First off, you'll all get a bath," was his first
statement, and it was greeted with thunderous cheer. "Next, you'll get
deloused," was followed by more cheering. The whole airdrome shook
when the intelligence officer said, "and after we finish these other things,
you'll be sent home."
   When thoughts were collected, the men relaxed. The trucks were

waiting to take the men off to reception centers for their bath and delousing. A thousand different stories of adventure, hardships, thrills, and confinement began to unfold.

2nd Lt. Robert Buckwalter, 1489 Locust St., Pasadena, Calif., B-17 navigator who went down over Ploesti in May said, "I can't tell anyone how glad I am to be free again and I don't believe any person in the world who hasn't had a similar experience can ever know how much it means to us. The conditions weren't too bad over there, but still, there's a feeling of uncertainty, loneliness, homesickness and futility that makes you lie awake nights waiting for the war to end, or for such a day as this."

Most of the men said their living conditions and food weren't as bad as they first thought they would be. Men who went down over Rumanian targets during the first Ploesti low-level attack of 1 August 1943 and others on up into May of 1944, found conditions quite poor until the great assault on the Ploesti field opened up and new crewmen were coming into the camp almost every week.

Previous to that time, the Rumanians had been rather unprepared. The food had been poor, treatment had been harsh at times, and living conditions were not all they might have been.

Later on, although the Rumanians themselves did not have any too large a food supply, the meals of the prisoners picked up in quality and in quantity.

Downed in May: T-Sgt. Robert J. Whoon, 2510 Riverside Drive, Houston, Texas, B-1; radio operator who went down over Ploesti in June said, "We had good cots to sleep on with straw-filled mattresses. While I was there the weather was warm and we each had one blanket, just enough to keep us comfortable at night. Most of the food was of a local type, not much meat, but enough to keep us filled up. Some of the guards could be bribed, and they'd bring us in some wine. Our camp, on the whole was

pretty cool. However, I understand a few of the boys in others nearby
suffered from malnutrition."

Officers Paid: 1st Lt. Marvin Lorder, 70 Brunswick Blvd., Buffalo,
N.Y., B-0 bombardier who went down over Ploesti the latter part of April
said, "Since most of the officers were paid a little each month, our food was
pretty good. We understood the enlisted men weren't doing as well so we
got up a fund, put some pressure on the authorities, and had better meals
prepared for the men. Most of us suffered vermin of one type or another,
as the delousing process the Rumanians put us through didn't seem to do
much good."

Rumanian soldiers guarded the enclosures the Americans occupied.
A few British and Russian soldiers were in the same camp. Every now and
then, German officers would carry out an interrogation of the men, and a
few were sent to Germany for interrogation and then returned to Rumanian
camps.

S-Sgt. John E. Cashan, 268 Mason Ave., Patterson, New Jersey, B-
17 tail gunner who went down over Ploesti in April said: "all hell broke
loose one night in August when our Rumanian guards notified us that
Rumania had capitulated. The next morning the doors were thrown wide
open and we were allowed to go any place we wanted. Many of the
Rumanian civilians came to the camp bringing melons, wine, bread, and
other types of food."

Journal Entry: 4 September

Target: Geno Harbor

The 817th was loaded with Block Busters—one bomb on each side
of the bomb bay. A huge bomb weighing three ton is armed with the
control device. When the bomb goes down through the cement pens it sets
off the bomb. We come in low at 17,000 feet to make sure these eggs hit

the target. As the bombs drop we quickly pull up into the air so flak is below us. We have hit the target!"

Journal Entry: 5 September
Target: The rail yard in Budapest Rail Yard.
We hit our target dead on. THAT should take care of the Germans and their supplies, and help the Red Army as they advance.

Journal Entry: 10 September
Target: An Oil Refinery in Vienna, Austria
Flak is Heavy. We see one B-17 go down.

Boat ride to Isle of Capri

Journal Entry: 11-15 September

We leave for rest camp in Rome. We climb on the GI truck that has seats on the railing on each side. Rome is about 200 miles from Foggia, so it will be a long trip. We make good time on the flat land but when we hit the hills the driver has to start shifting down as we start up the hill. This "hill" is about as high as the Rocky Mountains. We circle around the hill once before we start down.

We are dropped off at the quarters that were built for the Italian army, just across the street from the Coliseum. Very nice. Hot and cold showers. Good cots to sleep on.

Journal Entry: 14 September

On our first day of R & R, we wake up at 1000 hours. We wish for breakfast to magically appear but it doesn't, so we turn over and sleep another hour. I wake up, shave, and take a nice, long, hot shower. This feels good—so good I'm like a new man.

Our stomachs are grumbling and can no longer be ignored, so we all head for chow. Afterwards we take a walk down towards the coliseum. We meet a man with a horse and buggy taxi and take a ride around the town. We drive through an arch that separates the new part of Rome from the old part of the city.

Our first stop is at a sidewalk café for some Vino and enjoyed some delicious, little cakes made from barley. The only real way to see Rome is on foot, so we go for a walk. The statue of Moses by Michelangelo impresses me the most.

The next morning, this farmer is up at the crack of dawn. I hail myself a Fiat to take me to Vatican City. He leaves me off by the courtyard. It is a beautiful walk to the Vatican, with the doves coming down to feed. I walk through the front door and past the statue of St. Peter. I notice that his foot is broken off and is just a stub. As I stand there staring at the foot, a Swiss guard comes up and welcomes me. He explains that the foot needs to be replaced about every two years, but since the war, they can't get the material to replace it.

I look around. I watch as some poor, old women slowly climb the stairs to the cathedral. I follow them into a room where they kneel by a railing. They place their rosaries on the railing and wait. I'm not Catholic, so I don't know what they are waiting for, but I wait with them. Soon, the Pope comes into the room. I am honored as he shakes my hand and thanks me for coming. He speaks seven different languages as he blesses the rosaries, before going out onto his balcony.

I get back to our room and tell my buddies that I just shook hands with the Pope. My buddy, Filz, who is a nice Catholic boy from Appleton, Wisconsin, says, "Boy, you have some of the biggest stories ever!" I can see he doesn't believe me, so I challenge him: "Get your rosary beads and we'll go there tomorrow morning. Be ready by 0500."

The next day, Filz and I head back into town. I love to walk in the town or anywhere else. We get to St. Peter's Cathedral and wait in the same little room that I was in the previous day. Along with everyone else in the room, he puts his rosary on the rail, and sure enough, the Pope comes in, blesses his beads, and shakes his hand. Being a nice, Catholic boy, Filz is very excited. But even though I'm not Catholic, I still think it's a one of the greatest feelings and events I have had in my life. I mean, it helps you, no matter what church you go to. I think you just feel something special.

The next day we took a day trip to site see on the Isle of Capri. We enjoyed a lazy day of sight seeing and sampling the local foods.

Journal Entry: 17 September
We are back at Sterperone Air Base Shortly after chow Colonel

Sperry had us all fall out for formation and an impromptu awards presentation.   I am honored to be presented the Air Medal with three Bronze Clusters. The Air Medal signifies I have flown ten missions and each Bronze Cluster signifies an additional ten missions. So far I have flown 40 missions. I also received an ETO (European Theater of Operation) ribbon with three Battle Stars, each signifying different regions that I flew missions in: Italy, Africa and Southern Europe.

Colonel Sperry presents my awards

Journal Entry: 22 September

Today I am flying with a different crew because they need a tail gunner. Our mission is to stop the flow of oil from going into Germany. We take off and go up through flak alley. We are getting shot up pretty bad and are having some engine problems. We are starting to lose altitude and realize I don't have intercom. I look at my oxygen tank gauge and see that it is shooting down to zero. I grab the little walk-around bottle of oxygen we keep in the back and start for the waist so I can get more oxygen, but when I crawl past the tail wheel I pass out. The waist gunner drags me and hooks me up to the oxygen as we started into a dive. I came to all of a sudden and I don't know what is going on. In my confusion, I start to head for the open door to bail out, but the waist gunner stops me and says, "Look down, look down!" When I look down, I see the Adriatic Ocean, and that knocks some sense into me. I quickly step back.

I'm not feeling so good now because of the lack of oxygen and really don't care what's going on. All of a sudden we hit the ground. The pilot has brought down the plane on a little air strip twenty miles from the front line that is reserved for emergencies. I'm still feeling sick. I jump out onto the ground because I don't know what else to do. I go around to the back of the tail and hang onto the tail. The pilot comes to check on me because he knows I had lost consciousness and wants to see how I'm doing. I say, "Yea, I'm okay. I just feel a little sick."

He tells me, "Walk around the plane and count the flak holes that are bigger than your fist." So that's what we start to do. We can see forty big holes in the top, and there are several big holes right where I would have been. I guess it was lucky that I had run out of oxygen and had left the tail position.

The plane is no condition to fly, so we have to sit and wait for a GI truck to come and get us. Finally it arrives and we all pile in and head back to base, which is a thirty mile trip over little, rusty, tough roads. We don't get back until 1000 hours and I feel lucky to be alive.

I walk back to my tent, and as I approach, I see my buddy, Russ Lemmon, sitting silently by my tent. He must have thought I was down for sure, because when he sees me he looks shocked. He jumps up and gives me a big hug. We are happy to be together again!

Exert from Stars & Stripes: Memmingen Raid: 1 November 1944
One of the war's most memorable air attacks, a raid by B-17s of the 483rd Bombardment Group on the Memmingen airdrome installations in southwestern Germany in July, was accorded the highest recognition on Wednesday, 6 September 1944, with the presentation of a Presidential Citation to this group. Although the raid resulted in 143 men being shot down, the damage to the enemy fighter formation was in even greater proportion. During the air battle, B-17 gunners accounted for 53 fighters destroyed, some gunners downing four enemy planes. Five more enemy aircraft were damaged and eight others considered probable. Once on the bomb run, the 12 Forts remaining in the formation dropped their bombs with devastating results as every major installation on the ground was destroyed. Seventeen enemy aircraft were destroyed on the ground together with four probables and fourteen damaged. The day's score for the 483rd was 101 enemy fighters destroyed or damaged.

Originally the 483rd was part of a formation of 167 Fortresses with fighter cover, briefed to destroy the installations at Memmingen a high priority target. Enroute to the target, poor weather played havoc with the groups, resulting in some of the B-17s returning to their base although some went to bomb a secondary target. The fighter escort was separated altogether from the bombers and the 483rd with its tiny formation of 26 planes proceeded to Memmingen, alone and unescorted.

Once inside Germany, the Forts encountered opposition that was to reduce their number by more than half. A formation of 75 German fighters attacked the rear planes in the formation and a minute later another 125 enemy fighters joined the attack. Bit by bit, the Fortress force was whittled down, as attacking from the rear and working forward, waves of FW-190s and ME-109s downed plane after plane in the formation. In the first attack, seven Forts were downed and five more were destroyed in the second. Finally the twelve remaining Forts reached the target and dropped their bombs. As they turned from Memmingen, twelve D-38s from the 1st Fighter Group appeared and joined the one-sided battle. Shortly after, the enemy planes, their ammunition virtually exhausted, broke away from the fight and the Forts returned to their southern Italy base.

Journal Excerpt: 15 November

This is a Lone Wolf Mission. We take the ball turret out and put a radar unit where the ball turret was. The weather is bad, but with the radar unit, we can bomb through the overcast skies or wherever we want to because we can see our target on the radar screen. Our mission, which is to take out an oil pipeline and stop the flow of oil to Germany, will take us over flak alley again. We have been flying through the clouds, which give us cover, but when we emerged from them, there are fighters waiting to try and shoot us down. Before they had a chance to react, we go back into the clouds, and with the help of the radar screen, we release our load. We hit the target dead on, which was what we set out to do. The cloud cover gives us a safe ride home.

Journal Entry: 24 November

It is the day before Thanksgiving, but, as usual, a sergeant wakes me up and takes me down to the mess tent for breakfast and then out to the flight line. R'key greets me and tells me that there is a rumor going around that the only difference between us and the 8th Air Force in England is that we have nothing but milk runs. The brass has upped their missions to forty-five and lowered ours to thirty-five.

We are scheduled to fly to Linz, Austria and this mission is expected to be a rough one. R'key is concerned about me. "Why don't you go on sick call," he suggests.

I hesitate only briefly before answering. "We are holding up take-off time." I answer by crawling in the tail again.

He shakes his head. "I knew you would go, so I put two pieces of armor plate on each side of you to help keep you safe." I can always count on R'key.

Just as we leave the runway we hear the pilot over the intercom. "Who loaded this plane? The tail feels heavy. I have to compensate for it." No one answered. Complete silence.

The flak is thick but I have ridden through worse. I can see three or four holes above me that let in daylight. Bombs away and we head back to the air base in Linz.

We come in for a nice landing. A sergeant in a jeep greets me. When I pile out the waste door he says, "Colonel Sperry wants to see you. Good news!"

I'm dropped off at headquarters. I go through the door of the orderly room and give Colonel Sperry a salute. He's a big man with a big smile. He says, "How would you like to be on your way back to the U.S.A.? The rumor you heard about is true. If you pack your bag quickly, I can get you and four others on a hospital boat that is pulling into Naples, Italy. Or," he encourages, "you can pull three more missions and I'll see to it you get the DFC (Distinguished Flyer Cross)."

I have flown a total of 47 combat missions. I'm tired and ready to go home. I say, "Sorry Colonel, you can keep your medals! Besides, you can't give me a good conduct medal until I have been in the service for a full year, and that won't happen until December 7th. If the boat don't sink, I'll be home for Christmas, 1944."

Of course, I'm not one to leave without the last word. I had heard about the time Sperry had partied with his pals and some cheap whiskey, wrapping up the evening by buzzing some straw stacks. Unfortunately he flew a little too low. "If you fly into Africa for Christmas cheer, on the way back, don't buzz the straw stacks in Italy! My friend R'key doesn't like to pull the straw out of the engines!"

The next morning we were on our way to Naples by GI truck.

R ETURN TO THE STATES

November 1944

It is late afternoon when we arrive at Mussolini's race track. There is a stadium, and the grounds leading up to it are covered with pup tents. We are given a pass number, and how nice, it's starting to rain. I'm so glad to be leaving Italy. There are so many poor people here. Hungry people. Homes destroyed. Rail yards destroyed. As I stand here with a smile on my face, I feel so undressed. I have left my 45 revolver and my trench knife, which was always strapped to my right leg, at the base. I take my mess kit to the chow hall, and after filling my stomach, I go back and crawl into my pup tent. I am exhausted and immediately fall asleep.

The next morning the bugle blows for chow. It is Thanksgiving day, 1944. We enjoy a Thanksgiving feast; a piece of dry turkey, dehydrated potatoes, applesauce and a piece of ice cream which was made from condensed milk. But when you're hungry, you'll eat anything.

The next day we are still waiting for them to tell us it is time to go home. I'm in the first row of tents, so I am one of the first to be called to board the hospital boat that has a big, red cross on the side. We are all given numbers that tell us where our hammocks are; my number says I am on the top one. The whistle blows and we are on our way to the U.S.A.

We sail out into the Mediterranean and down past the coast of Africa. The weather is beautiful. The medical boat is not luxurious, like a cruise ship, but I am able to take a stroll around the ship and get some fresh air. I run into Gregory, and he tells me that Lemmon is flying home after flying his fifty missions and earning his DFC, and that Foster is next on to the list to fly home. It's great to hear the good news!

We are bored. Fortunately Gregory has his pinochle deck, so we decide we can spend some time out on the deck playing cards and enjoying the scenery. We soon pass the Rock of Gibraltar and are now out on the Atlantic Ocean.

We meet up with our convoy, which is one merchant ship, one destroyer, and one oil tanker. We run a zigzag course across the Atlantic to avoid detection by enemy subs. We head out one way, and then the other, as we head towards the U.S.A. We have smooth sailing and beautiful weather. I like to go on deck and watch the sun go down.

Twenty-one days into the cruise, as I'm leaning against the guard rail, I notice a G.I. with one leg off above the knee, and one arm missing just above his elbow. Limping on one crutch, he comes up and leans on the railing beside me. He asks, "How long have you been in the army?"

I thought about it a moment. "When we are out to sea for one more day, I will have a year in. It will be nice to get my good conduct medal!"

He laughs. "You fly boys are something else!"

The next night we meet again. He is very sad and I ask him what is troubling him. He tells me that just before he left the hospital he got a Dear John letter. "My girlfriend is going steady with my cousin, who is a farmer with a hundred cows." I put my arm around him and together we cry.

The next evening, as I come out on the deck, I see him by the railing. I walk his way, but before I can say hello, I see him pitch himself over the railing into the ocean. I run to the rail screaming, "Man overboard!" The sea was starting to get rough and I can't see him anywhere.

The sailors are quick to blow the whistle and to assemble. All eyes are looking overboard as we try to see him bobbing in the ocean, but we can't locate him. The medical boat makes one circle around, but we can not find him. The boats are just going too fast. They quickly catch up to the rest of the convoy and stay in formation. There is no time to stop. We turn and continue on the zigzag course as the convoy moves full steam ahead.

The next day, during roll call, his name is called. There is no answer. After supper when we are all resting in our hammocks, an orderly comes in and calls his name. One guy says, "I know where he is." The orderly rushes over to him. "He went to town!" Everyone laughs. I stop him on the way out and tell him what happened.

It is still good sailing weather, but the crew is getting nervous. One of them tells me, "We are going to run into a North Atlantic storm coming down from New York. Sure enough, the next day the waves start to get bigger. Those who can't take it get seasick. Gregory and I don't let a rocking and rolling boat slow us; we go down for chow.

The cook says, "What do you two flyboys want?"

"We want to eat dinner!"

"Nobody is eating until our stomachs get used to this up and down." He sounds like my Grandpa.

The next day there are even bigger waves. You can see the ship's propeller as it comes out of the wave. Before we hit the next wave, as the propeller goes down, I can just get a glimpse of the shoreline and the Statue of Liberty. It is a day before we can dock, as we have to wait until the other ships in the harbor leave. Finally it is our turn, and by the time we pull into dock, we all have our gear packed and are leaning on the top rail waiting to disembark. There is an army band standing by the gangplank.

The conductor yells, "What would you like to hear?"

We all shout, "*In the Mood*", and the band plays for us as we march off the boat! We stand aside as the wounded and casualties are carried off the boat and put in ambulances. We're put on a tugboat and sail across the bay past the Statue of Liberty. What a wonderful feeling to be alive!

Those of us who are able to walk on our own will stay overnight in New York. Tomorrow morning we will head to Walter Reed Hospital in Washington DC. It's getting dark as we enter the GI barracks. We pick out our sacks and drop our bags. I say to the guys, as we look down the street, "You see that long red beer sign? That means they have Miller High Life beer! That is where we are headed." We don't even take time to unpack before we are out the door and walking across the street. When we have drunk our fill, we head back to the barracks. We are just dozing off when we hear a PFC doing his business in the corner instead of in the latrine. The old sergeant says, "What is the matter with him? Isn't he housebroken?"

L EAVE

December 1944

The next morning we are on the train for Washington DC. As we are in line getting off the train, a photographer from the Washington Post takes our picture. "Home for Christmas 1944."

We are taken over to Walter Reed Hospital. They weigh me in at one hundred forty seven pounds. I have lost thirty-seven pounds! The doctor is checking our lungs, as being on oxygen thins our blood. I was not in very good shape and had war fatigue. Greg was also worn out. The doctor decided to give us both a fifteen day route delay, which meant we were going home! I was told that after my leave, I was to report to a convalescent hospital in Richmond, Virginia, to build my strength back up.

Home, for both of us, is Wisconsin. I turn to Greg. "Let's not waste any time here." We check the train schedules and find we can get a train to Chicago in an hour. We quickly find a taxi to take us to the train station, but when we arrive, there is a long line at the ticket booth, and it doesn't look promising. I notice that there is a guard at the gate that lets the people board the train. I approach him.

"Hey Mac, we need help to get our tickets and through the gate to the club car. I'll give you a carton of cigarettes if you can help us out." His eyes light up, as cigarettes are rationed and hard to get. He gets us our ticket and lets us through the gate as the crowd puts up a roar. He says to them, "I have special orders to get these two returning soldiers on the train!" As the train is backing into the loading platform, we hand him his carton of cigarettes.

We walk into the club car and flash another carton of cigarettes at the waiter, telling him that if he can get us an immediate table, the cigarettes are his. He whisks away the carton and we were soon sitting at a table and enjoying our Millers. The waiter brings us each a bowl of soup. We try to get a spoonful to our mouths but can't manage it as the table is shaking so badly. We tell the waiter, "Forget the soup and bring on the chow!"

By the time we have had an after dinner drink, we are in Chicago, just in time for us to catch our train to Green Bay. When the train stops in Plymouth, I bid Greg goodbye and a Merry Christmas.

Irmin Porke, who has a taxicab, is at the train station. "Where are you headed?"

"I need a ride to Schultz's tavern". I walk into the tavern. The bartender can't believe I'm back from overseas. My buddy, Tiny Miller, happens to be at the bar. He lifts me up in the air, as he is so happy to see me. After a couple beers, I asked Tiny if he will to take me to see my folks at Hall's Crossing, which is halfway between Plymouth and Fond du Lac.

I get home and wake up my folks. I hadn't told them I was coming, so they were really surprised and happy to see me. After lots of hugs, they started asking questions about the war. I pulled out a little hand book that was given to me. I showed them where it said, "Keep your mouth shut, the enemy is listening." They understood that I wasn't supposed to say much about what was going on. It has been a long day and I soon go up to bed. I look around the room and see that everything is as I left it.

I sleep long and deep, not waking until ten a.m. the next morning. Although Mother has made a delicious dinner, I can only eat just a little of everything before I am full.

After dinner, I call the Sheboygan Falls High School, where my girlfriend, Ethel, is a senior. She is so happy to hear my voice and starts to cry. We arrange to meet by her locker in a few minutes. When she sees me coming down the hall, she runs into my arms, plying me with hugs and kisses. This is the day I dreamed about when I was flying on missions.

Ethel works in the principal's office after school, so I make a date for later on. "I'll pick you up at seven and then we can go down to Mike Ten's, the local drug store and soda shoppe."

On the way to Ethel's house, I stopped at Kleinhan's Tavern in Plymouth. The room is full, but there is one stool at the bar, so I move in. Mrs. Kleinhans sees me and runs into the back to get her husband. He pours me a cold Miller High Life draft, sets it in front of me, and then goes back to the other end of the bar.

My friend next to me at the bar explains. "Remember their son,

Oh, I'm perfectly comfortable. I've been a gunner for years!

Merlin? Well, he was at the invasion of Anzio and took a bullet between the eyes." I told him that we lost over two thousand guys during that invasion. I drink up my beer and head out the door. I sat down on the steps with my head in my arms and tears in my eyes.

The time goes fast and Christmas day is here. I drive down to the farm and pick up Ethel to join the Holbrook family for our traditional

Christmas dinner. All the men in the family tell me that I am lucky to have a girl like Ethel! I sit down to eat and put a little of everything on my plate. It seems I just get started eating and all at once, I'm full. Everyone looks at me. "Can't you eat anymore?"

After dinner I sit with my cousins and they, too, starting asking questions about the B-17 and what combat was like. Again, I pull out my little handbook and tell them I have to keep my mouth shut. So instead, we just shoot the bullshit that makes the grass grow green, just like old times.

I told everyone that I appreciate how all the local farmers put in such long hours to provide food for us, and how it is helping us win this war. I am especially proud of my dad for winning an award at the county fair, recognizing him as the farmer who has increased milk production the most in his dairy herd. I tell them about all the starving people in Italy and Africa and how they are always begging for food. Just before I left Italy, a boat load of barley came into Naples from the U.S.A. to feed the starving people. At four o'clock, everyone leaves for home.

Two days later I leave for Richmond, Virginia. So much for Christmas 1944. My folks and Ethel take me to the train station in Plymouth. When I go to get my ticket, I pass a four-wheeled baggage cart. On top there is a rough box on it; it has Merlin Kleinhan's name on it. Tears again come into my eyes. I proceed onward to get my ticket on this very cold December day.

The train pulls into the station and it is time to kiss my mother and Ethel and to give my Dad a hug. The conductor takes my ticket and guides me to my seat. I look around and everyone is crying, for it is a sad goodbye. Who knows what is in store for us next?

In Milwaukee I catch the North Shore train that runs from Milwaukee to Chicago. I change trains in Chicago to Washington DC and then catch a bus from there to Richmond, Virginia. Time to convalesce!

R & R
Miami Beach, Florida

The medic takes one look at me, all one-hundred-forty-seven pounds, and says, "You need to go to Miami Beach for some Rest and Relaxation. "The next thing I know, I am on a fast train to Miami. I arrive at midnight, where I find that my buddy, Russ Lemmon, is also in Miami for R & R, and he is there to meet me with a taxi. We head out to a hotel on the beach, which has been taken over by the military for the sole purpose of having a place for soldiers to rest.

I wake at ten o'clock the next morning. I go to the window and look out. It is a bright, sunny day and sun is shining on the beach which sprawls directly below my window. A lot of sun-bathers are soaking up the sun. I must have died and gone to heaven! The phone rings and Russ is on the line. He and my buddy, Abi, pick me up and we go to dinner at some high class restaurant.

A week goes by. It is a Monday morning, January 8, 1945. A sergeant stops me and wants to know if I read the bulletin board. I said, "Where is it?"

He points. "You walk right past it every morning at ten o'clock before you go out and get into the car with your buddies." He tells me it's time to get back to work and gives me a choice of reassignments. I can either go back on the B-24 in the South Pacific or I can be a smoke jumper.

The Japs have been sending incendiary bombs that are landing in the forests in the west coast and the smoke jumpers are there to put out the fires. I remember one of my relations telling me about the big fire in Pestigo, Wisconsin and how hot it was and all that, so I tell him, "No, I don't want to be a smoke jumper. I guess I'll go back to the south Pacific."

I needed to be checked out by the medics before I could be released so they took me over. They look me over. I am underweight, my stomach is causing me problems and I have a spastic colon. They conclude, "This man needs more than a week's rest. We're sending him to Bowman Field Convalescent Hospital in Louisville, Kentucky."

CONVALESCENSE
Louisville, Kentucky
January to March 1945

The train I am on runs through Gasdon, Alabama. At the station, a sergeant from the Eighth Air Force boards the train. I stop him as he walks by and invite him to sit down to shoot the bull. His name is Milton Garrott. It turns out he is going to the same place I am. He got a piece of flak just below his eye. During surgery, they took out his eyeball, removed the piece of shrapnel from it, and put it back in again. He can see good now.

As we pull into the station at Louisville after chow, the ticket conductor yells, fall out for "Lucifer". Louisville is known as the land of fast women and beautiful race horses. Milton says, "How can we be so lucky?"

We take a taxi to Bowman Field. We stop at the gates and an MP comes out to check our orders. It's Walter Brickner from my home town! He looks over my orders and says to the other MP, "It looks as if we've got double trouble here!" The taxi takes us on to headquarters where we are assigned our barracks and cot numbers.

I'm on the second floor of our barracks and my cot is in the middle of the room. What a crew! The guy in the bunk across from me was shot down while his crew was bombing a town ahead of Patton's advancing forces. He lost his leg above his knee when he bailed out of his plane. The wind took him behind battle lines. The guy on the cot next to me shot down two German air torpedo bombers coming in on the boat he was on and he landed in the sea. He never flew a mission on a B-17. How am I supposed to get well in a ward like this, where everyone is moving around all night and noisy, keeping me from sleeping?

After a couple of weeks I am bored. I grab Milton and we go to downtown Louisville in a taxi. As we pass by the gate, Walter shakes his head. I tell the taxi driver to let us out at the best bar in town. He brings us to The Horse Collar, where the telephone is in a horse collar on the wall.

We drink a couple of beers, then we go out for a walk to see what is all happening on the downtown square. We stop at the theater to see what is playing. A band called Spike Jones and the City Slickers was playing music. As we were deciding whether or not to take in the show, a photographer walks up to us and asks us if we want to go with him to shoot a publicity picture with Spike Jones for the Louisville paper. He promises us that afterwards he would get us box seats for the afternoon show.

We head back to Spike's dressing room. He's no more than four feet tall, though he stands up on a bench so he can put his arms around us

Milton, Spike & I

for the photo shoot. The picture is to come out in the next day's paper. As promised, we get box seats for his show.

Afterwards, we go for a walk. As we pass a liquor store, we glance in and see a case of whiskey for $20; not a bad price for the good stuff. I tell Milton that I have some flying money in my wallet, so I buy a case to bring back to the barracks. The clerk calls a taxi for us and we head back to base. We slip in the side door with the case of whiskey, so as not to get caught.

Together we drink the whiskey and drown our sorrows. There is one guy who can't have any whiskey, which is understandable, because he only has half a stomach. So we put him on guard duty in case we get rowdy. That way, if an officer shows up, he can forewarn us. It doesn't take too long before the guys are singing and having a hell of a good time!

All of a sudden our guard yells, "Here come the brass!" I quickly gather the bottles and put them back in the case, lift the lid of the foot locker, shove the case inside, and slam the trunk lid shut. Those who are able to, quickly come to attention. As the brass walks down the rows they have to help some of the guys back into bed, checking footlockers as they go. The guy next to me is standing at attention with sweat running down his face. They check him over good, as well as his foot locker. They come to me. I stand at attention. One of the captains looks me directly in the eye. "What do you have to say for yourself?"

"I can't get any sleep around here with these clowns singing and dancing around," I gripe.

The captain continues down the row, sporadically checking foot lockers. He comes back and stands by me. He addresses everyone as he warns us, "We know you have whiskey hidden somewhere around here and we're going to find it!" He turns and walks out the door.

There is not a lot to do around here and I'm really bored. I'm in the infirmary about every three days while they check my stomach and colon, and monitor my weight. They tell me that my only job right now is to get stronger, and I am slowly gaining weight, but I'm also going crazy! It's time to get out of here!

I put in a request to transfer. They actually listen and send me to Denver to a photography school on board a B-20. I am soon on my way.

R ETRAINING
Denver & Fort Meyers
April to August 1945

The war in Europe continues. My job is to learn how to install and use the new camera equipment they want to install on the B-29s. The cameras will take pictures of the bomb strike site to know whether or not the strike is successful.

By May all my classes are over. I have learned how to use the new equipment and the Lieutenant tells me that they are sending me to Fort Meyers to install the equipment. I am leaving first and then a B-29 is to follow in a couple of weeks with the new photography equipment. When it arrives, I am to show one group how to install the equipment on the plane, and then another group how to use the equipment.

On May 8th, I am on a train on my way to Fort Meyers. We hear that the war is over in Europe. By the time I reach the next stop, we read about it in the papers, and everyone is celebrating.

After I arrived in Fort Meyers, I take a taxi out to the airbase and they take me over to the receiving squadron. Because the planes and equipment will not arrive for a couple of weeks, they have to find me something else to do.   •

The Lieutenant puts me in charge of fifty men from the 8th air force that had been based in England. They have each had two to five combat missions over Germany, so they think they know it all. They won't listen to me or keep their beds or the barracks picked up. I am frustrated, as this is new to me, so I asked for some help from the orderly room. They laugh at me and say, "You're a Sergeant. Just use your authority."

I go back to the barracks and firmly tell the men what to do. They laugh at me, too! I tell them I'm going over to see the camp Colonel. They laugh and boo me on my way out the door. I go over to headquarters and ask for ten minutes of the Colonel's time. I go in and give him a salute. I tell him that I want him to pull an inspection at 0100 hours while the men are still sleeping in their bunks. He rises up, shakes my hand, and assures me that he will be there.

At 0100, true to his word, the Colonel arrives with a Captain and a Lieutenant. We go to the first barracks. I step in the door and holler "Attention!" We are greeted with a big laugh, which immediately turns to dead silence as the Colonel steps in. The Lieutenant goes down each of the rows and writes each soldier up. They are put on KP for two weeks, and no passes off the base. I am not laughed at any more.

A B-29 finally arrives from Denver. When he sets down, the pilot makes a big belly on the runway. There is a lot of excitement as he taxis up and shuts off his engine. I greet the pilot, who is sweating profusely.

"Boy, I thought I was going to end up in the swamp", he says as he looks down the runway. "I think I can make it back out of here, though, as I will be lifting off from a different part of the runway."

The next week I am supposed to install the cameras in the B-29, so I am looking things over and making plans about how I will accomplish this. With both the camera and the gunner in the tail, there will be too much weight in the wrong place. It will make the plane off-balance and will be too dangerous. I tell them it won't work and I refuse to install the camera.

So the next day the plane leaves, and as the B-24 takes off, the pilot banks a twenty degree turn and his outboard engine quits. The plane crashes into the Everglades, killing all but one soldier. He was lucky because when the plane broke in half, he was airborne. As he came down he landed in a palm tree. He climbed down and walked away without an injury.

I am again out of a job, so they start retraining me on a B-29. My stomach is acting up again and I am often on sick call or light duty. Finally they put me on shipping orders for another assignment.

I'm not too keen on going back overseas. I know a WAC that takes care of the files in headquarters. She is on my side, and every time my name comes up to be shipped out, she slips my name to the back of the row again. It is looking like the war is closing down and I am hoping she can help me avoid going back until it is over.

I need to keep busy while waiting, so I get a job dealing black jack at the NCO club. I work three to four nights a week. The pay is not great, $10 a week, but the benefits are great—all you can drink!

My buddy, Lemmon, is also in Fort Meyers. He works as a MP. He stops by one night right before he goes on duty and sees me. I'm not dealing tonight, just having a drink.

"It'll be a long night, Holbrook. You'd better have another beer!" After a couple more, he tells me he needs to get the jeep from the motor pool, and as I have nothing better to do, I decide to tag along. He tells me to pop the bonnet and check the coolant in the radiator. After the hood is open and secure, I fill the water can with coolant and attempt to pour it into the little hole. I guess my aim isn't too good. Most of it misses the hole, instead hitting the blades of the fan, spraying one of the guards and covering him with coolant from head to foot. Apparently he doesn't have a very good sense of humor. He rewards me with a night in the cooler.

On another day, I ride along with Lemmon when he is on duty. We are taking some target practice at a long snake that is slithering along the side of the road. Using an M-1 rifle, I shoot it in the head. Lemmon and I have come up with a great idea! We hook a chain around the snake and drag it into camp and drop if off in front of the WAC barracks. The snake is sprawled across the sidewalk. We then drive around the side of the building to watch the fireworks.

When the WACs come out of their barracks they see the snake and they are all running around yelling and screaming. It isn't long before we hear on the jeep's radio that there is a snake outside the WACs barracks.

We quickly drive around the corner. The Calvary has arrived! Lemmon shoots the snake (again) and together we drag it away. Suddenly we are the heroes of the day!

We are killing time as we all wait for the war to end. We finally hear that the atom-bomb has been dropped on Japan. It is August 14th, 1945, a day to be remembered.

The enlisted men start to celebrate. They drink up all the beer in the PX and are headed for the Officer's Club. When they have drained the Officer's Club they head to the motor pool to take over the busses and head into town.

Our barracks is only for noncommissioned officers from Staff Sergeant to 2nd Lieutenant. We have our fifth of whiskey waiting to be opened the minute we hear Japan has surrendered.

All of a sudden, the barrack's door opens and in walk some MPs. They take us down to the main gates where we are handed a night stick. We are supposed to stop four busloads of celebrating enlisted men from going into town to celebrate. We took one look at the situation and decided the smartest thing to do is to open the gates and let the men go.

We wait three hours and then follow them in jeeps into town. We find the first bus by a bar. We go in and load the drunks into the bus. I have a truck driver's license so they have me drive the first bus load back to base. I drop them off at their barracks and usher them inside with no further incidents. They all make it back safely, but they don't get off scot-free. Their punishment is two week's of KP and they have to clean and paint the Officer's Club.

We all wait to hear when we can go home. We wait for the point system to work. All of us in our barracks have better than one-hundred-fifty points. We are listening to Drew Pearson on the radio and he reports that all men with more than one-hundred points are being discharged. So we call him up and tell him that we have more than one-hundred-fifty points and we are still here!

We tuned into his broadcast to find out what he had to say. He says, "The guys at Fort Meyers say they have more than one-hundred-fifty points, yet they're still there. Why is that? What's going on with the boys at Fort Meyers?"

The next morning a General and his staff fly into the base and close the whole base down. It's time to go home!

HOME FOR GOOD

November 1945

At Truax Field in Madison, Wisconsin, I wait in line to get my
discharge papers. When it is my turn, I step up, and here is Joe Ditters
from Plymouth, Wisconsin. He is typing out my discharge papers. It
doesn't take long and soon I have my discharge papers in my hand. I look
down at my discharge papers and read aloud.

Honorable Discharge
This is to certify that
John W. Holbrook, Staff Sergeant
2116th Army Air Forces Base Unit
Army of the United States
Is hereby Honorably Discharged from the military service of the United States of America
This certificate is awarded as a testimonial of Honest and Faithful Service to this country
Given at: Army Air Force Separation Base; Truax Field, Madison, Wisconsin
Date of Separation: 7 Nov 45

Enlisted Record and Report of Separation
Date of Induction: 29 Oct 43
Date of Active Service: 7 Dec 43
Service Outside Country: European Theater of Operation
Date of Departure: 13 Jul 44
Date of Return: 29 Nov 44
M.O.S.: Arial Gunner 611
Service Schools Attended: AAF Flexible Gunnery, Las Vegas, Nevada
Records and Citation: Rome-Arno, Southern France, Italian Campaign

Decorations and Citations: European, African, Middle Eastern Ribbon
Air Medal with 3 Bronze Clusters
General Order 2625 15th Air Force 17 Aug 44
Continental Service: 1 year, 5 months, 28 days
Overseas Service: 5 months, 3 days
Reason for discharge: Separation at the convenience of the government

Joe says, "I have been typing discharge papers for over a month and I've never seen anything that says MOS 611." I tell him we were the first class to graduate.

Joe fills me in with the final details. "Stop at the pay master and you will get $300 in discharge money, $100 in cash and a $200 check will follow in the mail. You are officially discharged!"

EPILOGUE

On My Own Again

I am now 84 years old. Life has been good to me. I remember back to when I first came home after the war. What a great feeling to be on my own and free again!

The first thing I did when I was discharged, was to go to Plymouth City Hall with my discharge papers. I joined the 52-20 Club, an organization for returning veterans. They gave us $20 a week for 52 weeks and helped us to find odd jobs until we got reestablished.

Kraft Cheese had cut back to its original crew and there were no available jobs. There were a lot of unemployed guys, so I considered myself lucky to be able to sign up with Mel Weiss to learn the mechanical trade under the GI bill. Mel owned Weiss Implement in Glenbeulah, and while the government paid me eighty dollars a month for two years while I was training, Mel paid me an additional $1.25 per hour to learn under his guidance. He knew everything from mechanics to plumbing, electricity, welding and much more!

I wanted to get an apartment so I could marry my Sunday girl, but there were no apartments available. In June, I heard that the lady who owned the Wade House in Greenbush was making an apartment upstairs. I immediately went and talked to her and she said it would be available on October 1st and she would rent it to me. The apartment was only a couple of miles from my job at Weiss implement.

With a place to live and means to a good living, it was time to marry my girl. Ethel and I got married on October 5, 1945 and we moved into our apartment above the Wade House in Greenbush, Wisconsin. I liked married life and Ethel and I had a good time getting to know the people in town.

I also was part of the VFW. We donated money for the junior football league and bought a tow line for the ski lift in Plymouth. We also got some land to be donated for the peewee baseball leagues. During the years there were always causes to support.

When my time was up, I got out of the service, but my friend Jimmy Foster reenlisted and eventually became a lieutenant. The last letter I sent him was when he was in Berlin and it came back marked "deceased".

Another friend, Jesse Allen, was also killed in action.

Gus Kroschewky was originally listed missing in action. He spent time in a POW camp but eventually made it home.

My buddy, Russ Lemmon, got out and moved back home to Charleston, West Virginia. He wanted me to come down to work at his

Below: My friend, Charley McGee at Air Show in Oshkosh, Wisconsin.

filling station or to work for his Dad in West Hamlet on the bus lines. He said he would put me to work right away, but I decided I wanted to stay in Wisconsin.

Lemmon later went back in the service; he finally got to be a pilot! Several years later, he was taking off in a B-25 and one of the motors seized and his plane cracked up. He was killed in the crash.

Over the years, I have been at a few reunions for the 483rd Bomb Group. They were in Minneapolis, Denver and Florida. It was always nice to see my old comrades-in-arms. The two friends I see most often are Gregory and Sonny Filz, as both are Wisconsin residents. Gregory lives up in Colfax and Sonny lives in Appleton.

I have also had an opportunity to meet members of the Tuskegee Air Squadron. During WWII, squadrons were still segregated. The Tuskegee's all black squadron flew over 15,000 missions, over 200 of them escorting heavy bombers. The Tuskegee's never lost a bomber and were the only squadron to hold that record. They were recently honored for their contribution to the war. A Tuskegee squadron flew escort for many of our missions. I have always been grateful to them for watching over me during our missions and keeping me alive.

It has been 63 years since my discharge from the Army Air Corps. Even though it was not even two years out of my life and we were just ordinary guys, it was an extraordinary time in our lives. The memories and the events that occurred during that time, the people that I met, and the friends that I made, have stayed with me to this day.

John at a 483rd Reunion

.

Printed in the United States
By Bookmasters